THE LLAMA EF

HOW META'S AI IS CHANGING THE WORLD

OLIVER LUCAS JR

Copyright © 2024 by Oliver Lucas Jr

All rights reserved. No part of this publication may be
reproduced, distributed, or transmitted in any form or by any
means, including photocopying, recording, or other electronic
or mechanical methods, without the prior written permission
of the publisher, except in the case of brief quotations
embodied in critical reviews and certain other non
commercial uses permitted by copyright law.

TABLE OF CONTENTS

Chapter 1

Chapter 2

Chapter 3

Chapter 4

Chapter 5

Chapter 6

Chapter 7

Chapter 8

Chapter 9

Chapter 10

Preface

The world is abuzz with the transformative potential of artificial intelligence. From self-driving cars to AI-powered medical diagnoses, the future seems to be unfolding at an unprecedented pace. But amidst the excitement and hype, it's easy to lose sight of the specific advancements that are driving this revolution. This book, "The Llama Effect: How Meta's AI is Changing the World," aims to shed light on one such advancement: Meta's LLaMA, a large language model poised to reshape how we interact with technology and each other.

This book is not just a technical deep dive into the intricacies of LLaMA (though we certainly delve into that!). It's an exploration of the broader impact of this technology, tracing Meta's journey from its social media origins to its current position at the forefront of AI innovation. We'll uncover the secrets behind LLaMA's impressive capabilities, examine its potential applications across diverse industries, and grapple with the ethical considerations that arise as AI becomes increasingly integrated into our lives.

Whether you're a seasoned AI researcher, a curious tech enthusiast, or simply someone interested in understanding the forces shaping our future, this book offers a comprehensive and engaging look at the LLaMA effect. We'll delve into the open-source revolution sparked by LLaMA, explore its potential to transform creative industries, revolutionize customer service, accelerate scientific discovery, and even redefine social connection.

But this book is not just about celebrating the potential of AI; it's also about acknowledging the challenges and responsibilities that come with it. We'll examine the potential biases embedded in AI systems, the importance of protecting privacy and security, and the need for ethical guidelines to ensure that AI is used for the benefit of all.

Ultimately, "The Llama Effect" is a call to action. It's an invitation to embrace the transformative power of AI while remaining mindful of its potential pitfalls. By understanding the capabilities and limitations of LLaMA, by fostering responsible AI development, and by engaging in open dialogue about the future we want to create, we can harness the full potential of AI to build a more equitable, sustainable, and fulfilling world for all.

Join us on this journey as we explore the LLaMA effect and its profound implications for the future of humanity.

Chapter 1

The Birth of LLaMA

1.1 Meta's AI Journey: From Facebook to the Frontier of Language Models

The story of LLaMA isn't just about a single language model; it's a chapter in the ongoing saga of Meta's evolution as an AI powerhouse. To understand LLaMA's significance, we need to rewind and trace the path that led Meta here, from its roots as a social media giant to its ambitions at the forefront of artificial intelligence.

The Early Days: AI at Facebook

Facebook, as it was known then, wasn't built on AI. Its initial focus was connecting people, and its early algorithms were relatively simple. Yet, even in those nascent years, the seeds of AI were being sown. The platform's explosive growth presented a unique challenge: how to personalize the experience for millions, then billions, of users. This is where AI began to play a crucial role.

Think about your Facebook News Feed. It's not a chronological list of every post from every friend and page you follow. Instead, it's a carefully curated selection, powered by AI, designed to show you the content you're most likely to engage with. This seemingly simple feature was a significant early application of AI at Facebook, using machine learning to analyze your interactions, predict your interests, and prioritize the content you see.

Beyond the News Feed, AI was quietly working behind the scenes in other ways. Facial recognition technology, also powered by AI, allowed for automatic tagging of friends in photos, making sharing and connecting even easier. And while perhaps less visible to users, AI was the engine behind Facebook's targeted advertising, analyzing user data and preferences to deliver relevant ads and drive revenue.

But Facebook's ambitions extended beyond applying AI to existing features. In 2013, the company established Facebook AI Research (FAIR), a dedicated research lab with a mission to push the boundaries of AI. Led by renowned AI researcher Yann LeCun, FAIR attracted top talent and focused on fundamental research in areas like computer vision, natural language processing, and machine learning. These early investments in research laid the foundation for Meta's future AI endeavors.

The Rise of Deep Learning

The early 2010s witnessed a revolution in AI with the rise of deep learning. This approach, inspired by the structure of the human brain, allowed for the creation of more complex and powerful AI models. Facebook was quick to recognize the potential of deep learning and embraced it wholeheartedly.

One of the defining moments in this era was Facebook's success in the ImageNet Challenge, an annual competition focused on image recognition. In 2013, a team from Facebook achieved a significant breakthrough, demonstrating the power of deep learning for computer vision tasks. This victory not only solidified Facebook's position as a leader in AI research but also paved the way for advancements in areas like object detection, image classification, and augmented reality.

Deep learning also fueled progress in natural language processing (NLP), the field focused on enabling computers to understand and generate human language. Facebook invested heavily in NLP research, developing models that could translate languages, analyze text, and even generate human-like text. This work culminated in the creation of M Translations, an AI-powered translation tool that facilitated communication across language barriers.

The rise of deep learning marked a turning point for Facebook. AI was no longer just a tool for improving existing features; it was becoming a core component of the company's strategy. AI-powered features were integrated into virtually every aspect of Facebook's products, from fighting misinformation and detecting harmful content to personalizing recommendations and enhancing user experiences.

The LLaMA Breakthrough

The culmination of Meta's AI journey, at least for now, is the development of LLaMA. This large language model represents a significant leap forward in AI, pushing the boundaries of what's possible with natural language processing. LLaMA's capabilities are vast, from generating creative text formats to translating languages with impressive accuracy.

But what truly sets LLaMA apart is its open-source nature. In a field dominated by closed-source models, Meta's decision to open LLaMA to the research community was a bold move. This decision reflects a commitment to democratizing AI, allowing researchers, developers, and even hobbyists to experiment with and build upon this powerful tool.

LLaMA's arrival signifies a new era for AI at Meta. As the company sets its sights on the metaverse, LLaMA is poised to play a pivotal role. Imagine AI-powered assistants that can seamlessly interact with users in virtual worlds, or AI tools that can generate immersive experiences and personalized content. LLaMA's open-source nature will foster collaboration and innovation, accelerating the development of these and other exciting applications.

Meta's AI journey, from its early days as a social media platform to its current position at the frontier of language models, is a testament to the company's commitment to AI research and development. LLaMA is not just a technological breakthrough; it's a symbol of Meta's ambition to shape the future of AI and its potential to transform our world.

1.2 Open Source Revolution: Why LLaMA is Different

The world of cutting-edge AI can often feel like an exclusive club, with powerful tools locked away behind closed doors. But Meta's LLaMA is rewriting the rules, ushering in a new era of open access and collaborative development. This open-source revolution is set to reshape the AI landscape, and understanding why LLaMA is different is key to grasping its transformative potential.

Walled Gardens

For years, the most advanced AI models have been held captive within the "walled gardens" of tech giants like Google and OpenAI. These companies, with their vast resources and talented teams, have produced impressive language models like PaLM 2 and the GPT series. But their insistence on keeping these models closed-source has created a bottleneck in AI progress.

Imagine a brilliant scientist with a groundbreaking idea, but no access to the necessary equipment to test it. This is the frustrating reality for many AI researchers outside these select companies. They are limited in their ability to study, experiment with, and build upon these cutting-edge models. Collaboration is stifled, innovation is slowed, and the potential for groundbreaking discoveries is diminished.

This restrictive approach is often driven by commercial interests. Companies invest heavily in developing these models, viewing them as valuable intellectual property and a source of competitive advantage. They fear that open access would erode their profits or allow others to build competing products. The result is a system where the pursuit of profit potentially overshadows the broader benefits that AI could offer to society.

Furthermore, the closed nature of these models creates a "black box" problem. We can marvel at their outputs – the impressive text, code, and translations – but we can't fully understand the intricate mechanisms that produce these results. This lack of transparency raises concerns about potential biases embedded within the models, making it difficult to identify and correct errors or unintended consequences.

These walled gardens, while producing remarkable achievements, ultimately constrain the potential of AI. They limit access, hinder collaboration, and obscure the inner workings of powerful tools. LLaMA, with its open-source philosophy, represents a radical departure from this status quo, offering a glimpse into a more open and collaborative future for AI.

LLaMA's Open-Source Approach

In a field dominated by secrecy and proprietary technology, LLaMA stands out as a beacon of openness. Meta's decision to release LLaMA as an open-source model is a bold move, challenging the prevailing norms and democratizing access to cutting-edge AI.

This open-source approach has profound implications for the future of AI. By making LLaMA's code freely available, Meta is empowering researchers, developers, and even hobbyists to experiment with and build upon this powerful tool. It's like opening the doors to a treasure trove of knowledge, inviting the world to explore, learn, and contribute.

This open access has the potential to accelerate innovation in the field of AI. With more minds working on LLaMA, identifying and addressing its limitations, and exploring its potential applications, progress is likely to be faster and more diverse. The collaborative spirit fostered by open source can lead to breakthroughs that might not have been possible within the confines of a walled garden.

Moreover, LLaMA's open-source nature promotes transparency and trust. Researchers can scrutinize the model's code, identify potential biases, and propose solutions. This open dialogue can help mitigate ethical concerns and ensure that AI is developed and deployed responsibly.

LLaMA's open-source approach is a breath of fresh air in the AI landscape. It's a testament to Meta's commitment to democratizing AI and fostering a more inclusive and collaborative future for the field.

1.3 Understanding the Technology: A Look Under the Hood of LLaMA

While LLaMA's open-source nature and potential impact are captivating, truly appreciating its significance requires peeking beneath the surface. This chapter delves into the technical intricacies of LLaMA, exploring the core components that make it tick and how they contribute to its impressive capabilities.

The Transformer Architecture: LLaMA's Foundation

At the heart of LLaMA lies a powerful neural network architecture known as the Transformer. First introduced in 2017, Transformers revolutionized the field of natural language processing with their ability to capture long-range dependencies in text, enabling a deeper understanding of language structure and meaning.

Imagine trying to understand a sentence where the key elements are separated by many words. Traditional neural networks struggled with this, but Transformers excel at it. They achieve this through a mechanism called "self-attention," which allows the model to weigh the importance of different words in relation to each other, regardless of their position in the sentence.

Think of it like reading a sentence with a highlighter, marking the words that are most relevant to each other. Transformers do this automatically, identifying the intricate relationships between words and phrases, even across long distances. This ability is crucial for understanding complex language and generating coherent and contextually relevant responses.

LLaMA builds upon this Transformer foundation, employing a decoder-only architecture. This means it focuses on generating text, predicting the next word in a sequence based on the preceding words. This is in contrast to encoder-decoder models, which are used for tasks like translation, where the encoder processes the input text and the decoder generates the output.

Tokens: The Building Blocks of Language

LLaMA, like other language models, doesn't process text as whole words. Instead, it breaks down text into smaller units called "tokens." These tokens can be words, parts of words, or even individual characters. This tokenization process allows the model to handle a vast vocabulary and capture the nuances of language.

Think of it like breaking down a sentence into Lego bricks. Each brick represents a token, and by combining these bricks in different ways, LLaMA can construct a wide variety of sentences and express diverse meanings. This flexibility is crucial for handling the complexities of human language, with its diverse vocabulary and intricate grammatical structures.

Layers Upon Layers: The Depth of LLaMA

LLaMA's architecture consists of multiple layers stacked on top of each other. Each layer performs a specific function, progressively refining the model's understanding of the input text. This layered structure allows LLaMA to capture increasingly complex patterns and relationships in language.

Imagine a detective analyzing a crime scene. They start with the most obvious clues, then gradually delve deeper, piecing together the evidence to form a complete picture. Similarly, each layer in LLaMA adds another level of analysis, extracting more nuanced information from the text.

These layers include:

Embedding layers: These layers convert tokens into numerical representations, capturing their meaning and relationships.

Attention layers: These layers employ the self-attention mechanism, allowing the model to weigh the importance of different tokens in relation to each other.

Feedforward layers: These layers process the information from the attention layers, further refining the model's understanding.

The number of layers in a language model significantly impacts its capabilities. LLaMA comes in different sizes, with varying numbers of layers, allowing for a trade-off between performance and computational resources. Larger models with more layers can capture more intricate patterns in language, but they also require more processing power.

Training Data: The Fuel for LLaMA

LLaMA's impressive capabilities are not solely due to its architecture; they are also a product of the massive dataset it was trained on. This dataset consists of a vast collection of text and code, encompassing books, articles, code repositories, and more.

Think of this training data as the fuel that powers LLaMA's engine. The more diverse and comprehensive the data, the better the model can understand and generate human language. LLaMA's training data is carefully curated to ensure quality and diversity, enabling it to handle a wide range of topics and writing styles.

Fine-tuning: Adapting LLaMA to Specific Tasks

While LLaMA is a powerful general-purpose language model, it can be further refined for specific tasks through a process called fine-tuning. This involves training the model on a smaller dataset tailored to the desired application.

Imagine a chef adapting a basic recipe to create a unique dish. Similarly, fine-tuning allows developers to adapt LLaMA to excel in specific areas, such as generating different creative text formats, translating languages, or answering questions in a particular domain.

This flexibility makes LLaMA a versatile tool for a wide range of applications. It can be used to power chatbots, generate creative content, assist with writing, translate languages, and much more.

By understanding the technical underpinnings of LLaMA, we can appreciate its significance as a major advancement in AI. Its Transformer architecture, tokenization process, layered structure, massive training data, and fine-tuning capabilities all contribute to its impressive performance and versatility. LLaMA is not just a powerful language model; it's a testament to the ingenuity of AI research and a glimpse into the transformative potential of this technology.

Chapter 2

The Power of Language Models

2.1 Beyond Chatbots: The Versatility of LLaMA

While the conversational abilities of large language models like LLaMA often steal the spotlight, their true power lies in their versatility. LLaMA is not just a chatbot engine; it's a multifaceted tool with the potential to revolutionize numerous fields, from creative writing and code generation to scientific research and education. This chapter explores the diverse applications of LLaMA, showcasing its adaptability and highlighting its potential to reshape our world.

LLaMA as a Creative Writing Partner

Imagine a world where writer's block is a distant memory, where ideas flow effortlessly onto the page, and where the creative process is amplified by an AI partner. LLaMA can make this a reality. Its ability to generate human-quality text makes it an invaluable tool for writers of all kinds.

Novelists can use LLaMA to brainstorm plot ideas, develop characters, and even generate entire scenes or chapters. Poets can explore new forms and styles, finding inspiration in LLaMA's unexpected word combinations and rhythmic patterns. Screenwriters can collaborate with LLaMA to craft compelling dialogue, develop intricate storylines, and even generate scripts for films or television shows.

LLaMA's versatility extends beyond traditional writing genres. It can be used to create compelling marketing copy, generate engaging social media posts, or even compose personalized emails. The possibilities are limited only by the user's imagination.

LLaMA: The Coder's Companion

The world of software development is also ripe for disruption by LLaMA. Its ability to understand and generate code makes it an invaluable tool for programmers of all levels.

Experienced developers can leverage LLaMA to automate repetitive tasks, generate boilerplate code, and even debug existing code. This frees up their time to focus on more complex and creative aspects of software development.

For novice programmers, LLaMA can serve as a patient tutor, providing code examples, explaining complex concepts, and even generating code snippets based on natural language descriptions. This can significantly lower the barrier to entry for aspiring developers, making coding more accessible and less intimidating.

LLaMA's code generation capabilities extend beyond traditional programming languages. It can be used to generate code for websites, mobile apps, and even embedded systems. This opens up new possibilities for rapid prototyping and development, accelerating innovation in the tech industry.

LLaMA: A Catalyst for Scientific Discovery

The potential of LLaMA extends far beyond the realms of creative writing and code generation. It can also be a powerful tool for accelerating scientific discovery.

Researchers can use LLaMA to analyze vast amounts of scientific literature, identifying patterns and connections that might otherwise go unnoticed. This can lead to new hypotheses, accelerate research progress, and even spark breakthroughs in various fields.

LLaMA can also assist in the drug discovery process, analyzing molecular structures, predicting drug interactions, and even generating novel drug candidates. This has the potential to revolutionize healthcare, leading to the development of more effective and personalized treatments.

Furthermore, LLaMA can be used to model complex systems, such as climate patterns or economic trends. This can help us better understand these systems, predict their behavior, and develop more effective solutions to global challenges.

LLaMA in the Classroom: A Personalized Learning Experience

Education is another area where LLaMA can have a profound impact. Its ability to understand and generate human language makes it an ideal tool for personalized learning.

Imagine a virtual tutor that can adapt to each student's individual needs and learning style. LLaMA can provide personalized feedback, answer questions in a clear and concise manner, and even generate customized learning materials.

LLaMA can also be used to create interactive learning experiences, such as simulations or games. This can make learning more engaging and effective, especially for subjects that students traditionally find challenging.

Furthermore, LLaMA can assist teachers in grading assignments, providing feedback, and even generating lesson plans. This can free up their time to focus on more meaningful interactions with students, fostering a more supportive and engaging learning environment.

The Future of LLaMA: A World of Possibilities

The applications of LLaMA are vast and continue to expand as the technology evolves. From generating creative content and assisting with coding to accelerating scientific discovery and personalizing education, LLaMA is poised to revolutionize numerous fields.

Its versatility stems from its ability to understand and generate human language, a fundamental skill that underpins countless human endeavors. As LLaMA continues to develop, we can expect to see even more innovative and transformative applications emerge, reshaping our world in ways we can only begin to imagine.

2.2 Natural Language Processing (NLP): The Engine of Understanding

Imagine a world where computers can not only process data but truly understand the nuances of human language, grasping the meaning behind our words, the emotions they convey, and the intentions they express. This is the realm of Natural Language Processing (NLP), a field of artificial intelligence that empowers computers to interact with human language in ways that were once considered science fiction. This chapter delves into the core concepts of NLP, exploring its evolution, its key techniques, and its pivotal role in powering LLaMA's impressive capabilities.

Deciphering the Code of Human Language

Human language is a complex and intricate system, filled with ambiguities, subtleties, and cultural nuances. For computers to truly understand it, they need to go beyond simply processing words as strings of characters. They need to grasp the underlying meaning, the context, and the intent behind our communication.

This is where NLP comes in. It equips computers with the tools to analyze, understand, and generate human language, bridging the gap between human communication and machine comprehension. NLP encompasses a wide range of tasks, including:

Text classification: Categorizing text into different categories, such as spam detection or sentiment analysis.

Information extraction: Extracting key information from text, such as names, dates, or locations.

Machine translation: Translating text from one language to another, preserving meaning and context.

Text summarization: Condensing large amounts of text into concise summaries.

Question answering: Providing accurate answers to questions posed in natural language.

Dialogue generation: Creating natural-sounding conversations between humans and machines.

These tasks, and many others, are the building blocks of NLP, enabling computers to interact with human language in increasingly sophisticated ways.

The Evolution of NLP: From Rule-Based Systems to Deep Learning

The journey of NLP has been marked by significant advancements, driven by evolving technologies and approaches. Early NLP systems relied heavily on rule-based methods, where linguists manually crafted rules to define grammatical structures and semantic relationships. While these systems had some success, they were limited in their ability to handle the complexities and ambiguities of human language.

The advent of statistical NLP in the 1990s marked a turning point. This approach leveraged statistical methods and machine learning algorithms to analyze large amounts of text data, identifying patterns and relationships that were not explicitly defined by rules. This enabled NLP systems to handle more complex language tasks and adapt to different language variations.

The recent rise of deep learning has further revolutionized NLP. Deep learning models, inspired by the structure of the human brain, can learn intricate patterns and representations from vast amounts of data. This has led to significant breakthroughs in NLP, enabling machines to perform tasks like machine translation and text summarization with unprecedented accuracy.

NLP Techniques: Unveiling the Toolkit

NLP draws upon a diverse set of techniques to analyze and understand human language. Some of the key techniques include:

Tokenization: Breaking down text into smaller units, such as words or subwords, to facilitate analysis.

Part-of-speech tagging: Identifying the grammatical role of each word in a sentence, such as noun, verb, or adjective.

Named entity recognition: Identifying and classifying named entities in text, such as people, organizations, or locations.

Sentiment analysis: Determining the emotional tone of a piece of text, such as positive, negative, or neutral.

Word embeddings: Representing words as numerical vectors, capturing their semantic relationships and contextual meanings.

These techniques, and many others, form the toolkit of NLP, enabling computers to dissect and interpret human language with increasing precision.

NLP: The Driving Force Behind LLaMA

LLaMA's impressive capabilities are deeply rooted in the advancements of NLP. Its ability to generate human-quality text, translate languages, and answer questions in a comprehensive and informative way is a testament to the power of NLP.

LLaMA leverages cutting-edge NLP techniques, such as deep learning and transformer networks, to achieve its remarkable performance. These techniques allow LLaMA to capture the nuances of human language, understand context, and generate text that is both coherent and relevant.

NLP is the engine that drives LLaMA's understanding of human language, enabling it to perform a wide range of tasks and interact with humans in a natural and intuitive way.

The Future of NLP: Towards True Language Understanding

The field of NLP continues to evolve at a rapid pace, with new techniques and applications emerging constantly. As NLP systems become more sophisticated, they are moving closer to true language understanding, where machines can not only process words but also grasp the underlying meaning, intent, and emotions behind human communication.

This progress has the potential to transform our interactions with technology, enabling more natural and intuitive communication with machines. From AI assistants that can understand our needs to chatbots that can provide empathetic support, NLP is paving the way for a future where humans and machines can communicate seamlessly.

2.3 Applications Across Industries: How LLaMA is Being Used Today

LLaMA, with its impressive language capabilities and open-source nature, is rapidly making its mark across diverse industries. This chapter explores real-world applications of LLaMA, showcasing how it's being used today to solve problems, improve efficiency, and drive innovation.

Education: Personalized Learning and Enhanced Accessibility

LLaMA is transforming education by enabling personalized learning experiences and enhancing accessibility for students with diverse needs.

Adaptive Learning Platforms: Educational technology companies are integrating LLaMA into their platforms to create adaptive learning experiences that cater to individual student needs. LLaMA can assess student understanding, provide personalized feedback, and generate customized learning materials, ensuring that each student receives the support they need to succeed.

AI-Powered Tutors: LLaMA can power virtual tutors that provide students with on-demand support and guidance. These tutors can answer questions, explain complex concepts, and offer encouragement, helping students overcome challenges and achieve their learning goals.

Accessibility Tools: LLaMA can be used to create tools that make education more accessible for students with disabilities. For example, LLaMA can generate text-to-speech and speech-to-text conversions, provide real-time captioning for videos, and even translate educational materials into different languages.

Customer Service: Efficient and Empathetic Support

LLaMA is revolutionizing customer service by enabling businesses to provide efficient and empathetic support at scale.

AI-Powered Chatbots: LLaMA can power chatbots that handle customer inquiries, resolve issues, and provide 24/7 support. These chatbots can understand natural language, provide personalized responses, and even escalate complex issues to human agents when necessary.

Automated Email Responses: LLaMA can generate automated email responses that are tailored to individual customer needs. This can significantly reduce response times and improve customer satisfaction.

Sentiment Analysis: LLaMA can analyze customer feedback to identify areas where businesses can improve their products or services. This can help businesses proactively address customer concerns and enhance their overall experience.

Content Creation: Generating High-Quality Content at Scale

LLaMA is empowering content creators to generate high-quality content at scale, freeing up their time to focus on more strategic tasks.

Marketing Copy: LLaMA can generate compelling marketing copy for websites, social media, and email campaigns. This can help businesses reach a wider audience and promote their products or services more effectively.

News Articles and Blog Posts: LLaMA can generate news articles and blog posts on a variety of topics, providing businesses with a constant stream of fresh content to engage their audience.

Creative Writing: LLaMA can assist writers in generating different creative text formats, such as poems, scripts, and even novels. This can help writers overcome creative blocks and explore new ideas.

Research and Development: Accelerating Innovation

LLaMA is accelerating innovation in research and development by enabling scientists and engineers to analyze data, generate hypotheses, and develop new solutions more efficiently.

Drug Discovery: LLaMA can analyze molecular structures, predict drug interactions, and even generate novel drug candidates, accelerating the drug discovery process and leading to the development of more effective treatments.

Scientific Literature Analysis: LLaMA can analyze vast amounts of scientific literature, identifying patterns and connections that might otherwise go unnoticed. This can lead to new hypotheses and accelerate research progress.

Code Generation: LLaMA can generate code for various programming languages, automating repetitive tasks and freeing up developers to focus on more complex and creative aspects of software development.

Other Industries: Expanding Horizons

The applications of LLaMA extend far beyond these examples. It is being used in a wide range of industries, including:

Healthcare: LLaMA can assist in medical diagnosis, patient education, and even mental health support.

Finance: LLaMA can analyze financial data, generate reports, and even provide investment advice.

Legal: LLaMA can assist in legal research, document review, and even contract drafting.

Manufacturing: LLaMA can optimize production processes, predict equipment failures, and even generate instructions for assembly lines.

As LLaMA continues to evolve and its capabilities expand, we can expect to see even more innovative and transformative applications emerge across all sectors of society. Its ability to understand and generate human language, coupled with its open-source nature, makes it a powerful tool for solving problems, improving efficiency, and driving progress in the years to come.

Chapter 3

LLaMA vs. the Competition

3.1 The AI Landscape: Comparing LLaMA to Other Language Models

The field of large language models (LLMs) is a bustling arena, with new contenders constantly emerging and existing ones evolving at a rapid pace. This chapter provides a comparative analysis of LLaMA, placing it within the broader AI landscape and highlighting its unique strengths and limitations compared to other prominent language models.

Key Players in the LLM Arena

Before diving into comparisons, let's introduce some of the major players in the LLM space:

GPT-3 and GPT-4 (OpenAI): These models, developed by OpenAI, have garnered significant attention for their impressive text generation capabilities. GPT-3, with its 175 billion parameters, was a groundbreaking achievement, and GPT-4 further pushes the boundaries with its rumored trillion parameters and multimodal capabilities.

PaLM 2 (Google): Google's latest language model, PaLM 2, boasts improved multilingual capabilities, reasoning skills, and code generation prowess. It powers Google's Bard chatbot and is integrated into various Google services.

Claude (Anthropic): Focused on safety and ethical considerations, Claude aims to be a "helpful and harmless AI assistant." It prioritizes avoiding harmful or biased outputs and engaging in helpful and informative conversations.

Bard (Google): Bard is Google's conversational AI service, powered by PaLM 2. It's designed to provide informative and comprehensive answers to a wide range of questions and engage in multi-turn conversations.

LLaMA's Distinguishing Features

LLaMA stands out in this crowded field due to a combination of factors:

Open-Source Nature: Unlike many of its competitors, LLaMA is open source, allowing for greater transparency, community-driven development, and wider accessibility.

Performance Efficiency: LLaMA is designed to be computationally efficient, requiring less processing power to achieve comparable performance to larger models. This makes it more accessible for researchers and developers with limited resources.

Focus on Research: While LLaMA has potential for commercial applications, its primary focus is to facilitate research in the field of LLMs. This encourages exploration, experimentation, and a deeper understanding of these powerful models.

Comparing Capabilities

While all LLMs share the ability to process and generate human language, they differ in their specific strengths and weaknesses.

Text Generation: LLaMA demonstrates strong performance in text generation tasks, comparable to GPT-3 in many aspects. However, GPT-4 and PaLM 2 may have an edge in generating more nuanced and creative text formats.

Reasoning and Logic: LLaMA shows promising capabilities in logical reasoning and problem-solving. However, models like

PaLM 2 and Claude may have an advantage in handling more complex reasoning tasks and providing more accurate answers.

Code Generation: LLaMA demonstrates proficiency in generating code in various programming languages. However, PaLM 2 is specifically designed with code generation in mind and may outperform LLaMA in this domain.

Multilingual Capabilities: LLaMA supports multiple languages, but models like PaLM 2 may have a broader language coverage and better performance in multilingual tasks.

The Trade-offs: Size vs. Efficiency

One key differentiator among LLMs is their size, measured by the number of parameters. Larger models, like GPT-4, tend to have greater capacity for learning and generating more complex outputs. However, they also require significantly more computational resources.

LLaMA takes a different approach, prioritizing efficiency over sheer size. It comes in various sizes, with the largest having 65 billion parameters, significantly smaller than GPT-3 or PaLM 2. This allows LLaMA to achieve impressive performance with less computational overhead, making it more accessible for researchers and developers with limited resources.

The Open-Source Advantage

LLaMA's open-source nature sets it apart from many of its competitors. This allows for:

Transparency: Researchers can examine LLaMA's code, understand its inner workings, and identify potential biases or limitations.

Community-Driven Development: The open-source community can contribute to LLaMA's development, fixing bugs, improving performance, and expanding its capabilities.

Accessibility: LLaMA is more accessible to researchers and developers who may not have the resources to train or access large, closed-source models.

The Evolving Landscape

The field of LLMs is constantly evolving, with new models and advancements emerging regularly. LLaMA, with its open-source nature and focus on research, is poised to play a key role in shaping the future of this exciting field.

By fostering collaboration, transparency, and accessibility, LLaMA is democratizing access to powerful AI tools and accelerating the pace of innovation. As the LLM landscape continues to evolve, LLaMA's unique strengths and contributions will undoubtedly shape the future of human-computer interaction and drive progress across various domains.

3.2 Strengths and Weaknesses: A Balanced Perspective on LLaMA

LLaMA, like any technology, is not without its limitations. This chapter offers a balanced perspective, exploring both the strengths that make LLaMA a compelling tool and the weaknesses that require careful consideration and ongoing development.

Strengths: Where LLaMA Shines

Open-Source Accessibility: LLaMA's open-source nature is a significant strength, fostering transparency, collaboration, and accessibility. This democratizes access to powerful AI technology, allowing researchers, developers, and enthusiasts to experiment, contribute, and build upon the model.

Performance Efficiency: LLaMA achieves impressive performance with a smaller model size compared to some competitors. This efficiency makes it more accessible for those with limited computational resources and reduces the environmental impact associated with training and deploying large language models.

Strong Foundation: LLaMA builds upon the robust transformer architecture, inheriting its strengths in capturing long-range dependencies and understanding complex language structures. This foundation ensures a solid base for LLaMA's capabilities in text generation, translation, and other language-based tasks.

Versatility: LLaMA demonstrates versatility across various applications, from assisting with creative writing and code generation to aiding in research and education. This adaptability makes it a valuable tool for diverse fields and use cases.

Active Research Community: LLaMA's open-source nature has fostered a vibrant research community, actively exploring its capabilities, identifying areas for improvement, and contributing to its ongoing development. This collaborative environment accelerates progress and ensures that LLaMA remains at the forefront of LLM research.

Weaknesses: Areas for Improvement

Potential for Misuse: As with any powerful technology, LLaMA can be misused for malicious purposes, such as generating harmful content, spreading misinformation, or creating deepfakes. Addressing these risks requires responsible development, ethical guidelines, and robust safeguards.

Bias and Fairness: LLaMA, like other LLMs, is trained on massive datasets that may contain biases present in the real world. This can lead to biased outputs or discriminatory outcomes if not carefully addressed. Ongoing research focuses on mitigating bias and ensuring fairness in LLaMA's applications.

Limited Explainability: While LLaMA demonstrates impressive performance, understanding the reasoning behind its outputs can be challenging. This lack of explainability can raise concerns in critical applications where transparency and accountability are essential.

Resource Requirements: While LLaMA is more efficient than some larger models, training and deploying it still requires significant computational resources. This can be a barrier for individuals or organizations with limited access to powerful hardware.

Ongoing Development: LLaMA is still under active development, and its capabilities are constantly evolving. This means that there may be limitations or areas where further improvements are needed.

A Balanced Perspective

LLaMA represents a significant advancement in the field of large language models, offering a compelling combination of performance, efficiency, and open-source accessibility. However, it's crucial to acknowledge its limitations and potential risks.

By maintaining a balanced perspective, recognizing both strengths and weaknesses, we can harness LLaMA's potential responsibly and effectively. Ongoing research, community collaboration, and ethical considerations will be essential in guiding LLaMA's development and ensuring its positive impact on society.

3.3 The Future of the Field: Where LLaMA Fits In

The landscape of large language models is dynamic and rapidly evolving, with new architectures, training techniques, and applications emerging constantly. This chapter explores the future trajectory of this exciting field and examines where LLaMA fits within this evolving landscape.

Trends Shaping the Future of LLMs

Several key trends are shaping the future of large language models:

Increased Scale and Efficiency: The trend towards larger models with more parameters continues, pushing the boundaries of language understanding and generation. However, there's also a growing emphasis on efficiency, with researchers exploring techniques to achieve comparable performance with smaller, more computationally efficient models.

Multimodality: LLMs are moving beyond text, incorporating other modalities like images, audio, and video. This allows for richer interactions and opens up new possibilities in areas like image captioning, video understanding, and even generating creative content across multiple modalities.

Enhanced Reasoning and Problem-Solving: Researchers are actively working on improving the reasoning and problem-solving abilities of LLMs. This involves developing new architectures and training techniques that enable LLMs to perform more complex cognitive tasks, such as logical deduction, common sense reasoning, and even scientific discovery.

Personalization and Customization: LLMs are becoming increasingly personalized, adapting to individual users' needs and preferences. This trend is driven by advancements in fine-tuning techniques and the ability to incorporate user-specific data into the models.

Ethical Considerations and Responsible AI: As LLMs become more powerful and pervasive, ethical considerations are taking center stage. Researchers and developers are focusing on mitigating bias, ensuring fairness, and promoting responsible use of these technologies.

LLaMA's Role in the Evolving Landscape

LLaMA, with its unique strengths and open-source nature, is well-positioned to play a significant role in shaping the future of LLMs.

Driving Open Innovation: LLaMA's open-source approach fosters collaboration and accelerates innovation by allowing researchers and developers to freely access and build upon the model. This democratizes access to powerful AI technology and encourages a more diverse range of applications and perspectives.

Pushing the Boundaries of Efficiency: LLaMA's focus on efficiency aligns with the growing trend towards smaller, more computationally efficient models. This makes it an attractive option for researchers and developers with limited resources and contributes to reducing the environmental impact of LLMs.

Facilitating Research and Experimentation: LLaMA's primary focus on research encourages exploration and experimentation, pushing the boundaries of LLM capabilities and contributing to a deeper understanding of these complex models.

Promoting Ethical Development: LLaMA's open-source nature promotes transparency and accountability, facilitating the identification and mitigation of biases and promoting responsible AI development.

Challenges and Opportunities

While LLaMA holds great promise, there are also challenges and opportunities that will shape its future trajectory:

Maintaining Momentum: The LLM landscape is highly competitive, with new models and advancements emerging constantly. LLaMA will need to continue evolving and improving to remain relevant and competitive.

Addressing Limitations: LLaMA, like other LLMs, has limitations in areas like reasoning, explainability, and bias mitigation. Addressing these limitations through ongoing research and development will be crucial.

Fostering Responsible Use: As LLaMA's capabilities grow, it's essential to ensure its responsible use and prevent misuse. This requires developing ethical guidelines, robust safeguards, and promoting responsible AI practices within the community.

Expanding Applications: LLaMA's versatility opens up a wide range of potential applications. Exploring and developing new use cases across diverse fields will be key to maximizing its impact.

A Collaborative Future

The future of LLMs is not just about individual models but about the collective efforts of researchers, developers, and the broader community. LLaMA, with its open-source philosophy, embodies this collaborative spirit.

By fostering open innovation, promoting responsible AI practices, and pushing the boundaries of LLM capabilities, LLaMA is poised to play a pivotal role in shaping a future where LLMs empower individuals, enhance productivity, and drive progress across various domains.

Chapter 4

LLaMA and the Creative Industries

4.1 Writing with AI: From Content Creation to Scriptwriting

The pen might be mightier than the sword, but in the digital age, the keyboard is king. And increasingly, that keyboard is being powered by artificial intelligence. This chapter explores the transformative impact of AI, and specifically LLaMA, on the craft of writing, from generating blog posts and marketing copy to crafting screenplays and even penning novels.

AI as a Creative Partner

Imagine a writing partner who never tires, never complains, and is always brimming with ideas. That's the promise of AI in the realm of writing. LLaMA, with its ability to generate human-quality text, can act as a tireless collaborator, assisting writers in various ways:

Overcoming Writer's Block: We've all been there - staring at a blank page, the cursor blinking mockingly. LLaMA can help break through those creative barriers by generating ideas, offering alternative phrasing, or even drafting entire paragraphs to get the creative juices flowing.

Exploring New Styles and Voices: Want to try your hand at a different genre or experiment with a new voice? LLaMA can help you explore those uncharted territories, providing examples and inspiration to expand your writing repertoire.

Boosting Productivity: LLaMA can handle the heavy lifting of content creation, generating drafts, outlines, and even entire articles, freeing up writers to focus on refining, editing, and adding their unique human touch.

Content Creation: From Blogs to Brochures

The applications of AI in content creation are vast and varied. LLaMA can be used to generate:

Blog Posts: Need to churn out engaging blog content on a regular basis? LLaMA can help you generate articles on a wide range of topics, complete with headings, subheadings, and even relevant images.

Marketing Copy: Crafting compelling marketing materials can be time-consuming. LLaMA can assist in generating website copy, social media posts, email newsletters, and even product descriptions, ensuring your message is clear, concise, and persuasive.

Creative Content: From poems and short stories to scripts and even novels, LLaMA can be a valuable tool for exploring creative writing endeavors. It can generate different text formats, experiment with styles, and even help you develop characters and plotlines.

Scriptwriting: Lights, Camera, AI!

The world of film and television is also embracing the power of AI. LLaMA can assist screenwriters in:

Generating Dialogue: Crafting natural-sounding dialogue is crucial for any screenplay. LLaMA can help generate conversations that are engaging, realistic, and tailored to specific characters.

Developing Plotlines: Struggling with plot twists or character arcs? LLaMA can offer suggestions, generate alternative scenarios, and even help you brainstorm new ideas to keep your story moving.

Creating Storyboards: LLaMA can even assist in creating visual representations of your script, generating descriptions that can be used to create storyboards or even rough animations.

The Human-AI Partnership

It's important to emphasize that AI is not here to replace human writers. Instead, it's a powerful tool that can augment and enhance the creative process. The most successful applications of AI in writing involve a collaborative partnership between human and machine.

The human writer brings their unique creativity, critical thinking, and emotional intelligence to the table, while AI provides the raw materials, the inspiration, and the efficiency to bring those ideas to life. This partnership allows writers to focus on what they do best: crafting compelling narratives, developing engaging characters, and expressing their unique voice.

The Future of Writing with AI

As AI technology continues to advance, we can expect even more sophisticated tools and applications to emerge in the realm of writing. LLaMA, with its open-source nature and focus on research, is poised to play a key role in shaping this future.

Imagine a world where writers can seamlessly collaborate with AI partners, where creative blocks are a thing of the past, and where the power of language is amplified by the intelligence of machines. This is the future of writing with AI, a future where human creativity and machine intelligence converge to unlock new possibilities and push the boundaries of storytelling.

4.2 Generating Images and Music with LLaMA

LLaMA is a powerful tool that can be used to generate images and music. It can be used to create abstract art, landscapes, portraits, and more. LLaMA can also be used to generate different styles of music, such as classical, jazz, and pop.

To generate images with LLaMA, you can provide a text description of the image you want to create. For example, you could say "Generate an image of a cat sitting on a chair." LLaMA will then use its knowledge of the world to generate an image that matches your description.

To generate music with LLaMA, you can provide a text description of the music you want to create. For example, you could say "Generate a piece of music that is sad and slow." LLaMA will then use its knowledge of music theory to generate a piece of music that matches your description.

LLaMA is a powerful tool that can be used to create art and music in a variety of styles. It is a valuable tool for artists, musicians, and anyone who wants to explore their creativity.

4.3 The Future of Entertainment: AI's Role in Movies and Games

Hold onto your seats, because the world of entertainment is about to be transformed by the power of AI. From the silver screen to the immersive realms of gaming, artificial intelligence is poised to revolutionize how stories are told, characters are brought to life, and experiences are crafted. This chapter explores the exciting future of entertainment, where AI, including models like LLaMA, takes center stage.

Movies Reimagined: AI in Filmmaking

Imagine a world where movie production is streamlined, creative barriers are broken, and audience experiences are personalized. AI is making this a reality, impacting every stage of filmmaking:

Scriptwriting and Story Development: AI tools can analyze scripts, suggest plot improvements, and even generate entire scenes or dialogue, assisting writers in crafting compelling narratives. LLaMA, with its language generation capabilities, can be a valuable partner in brainstorming ideas, developing characters, and overcoming writer's block.

Casting and Performance: AI can analyze actors' performances, identifying subtle nuances and emotional cues to assist in casting decisions. It can even be used to create digital avatars of actors, enabling them to portray characters beyond the limitations of age, appearance, or even mortality.

Visual Effects and Animation: AI is revolutionizing visual effects, automating tedious tasks, generating realistic environments, and even creating lifelike characters. This not only reduces production costs but also opens up new creative possibilities for filmmakers.

Personalized Experiences: AI can analyze audience preferences and tailor movie experiences to individual tastes. This could involve generating personalized trailers, recommending movies based on individual preferences, or even creating interactive narratives where viewers can influence the story's direction.

Gaming Redefined: AI in Interactive Worlds

The gaming industry is no stranger to AI, but the future holds even more immersive and intelligent experiences, thanks to advancements in AI technology:

Intelligent NPCs (Non-Player Characters): Say goodbye to repetitive and predictable game characters. AI-powered NPCs can exhibit more complex behaviors, adapt to player actions, and even engage in dynamic conversations, creating more realistic and engaging game worlds.

Procedural Content Generation: AI can generate game content on the fly, creating vast and varied worlds, unique quests, and even personalized storylines. This ensures that every playthrough is a unique and unpredictable experience.

Adaptive Difficulty: AI can analyze player skills and adjust the game's difficulty accordingly, ensuring a challenging but rewarding experience for all players. This prevents frustration for novice players while keeping experienced gamers engaged.

Immersive Storytelling: AI can enhance storytelling in games by creating dynamic narratives that react to player choices, generating personalized dialogue, and even adapting the game world based on player actions.

The Metaverse and Beyond: AI-Powered Entertainment

The future of entertainment extends beyond movies and games, into the emerging realm of the metaverse. AI will play a crucial role in creating these immersive virtual worlds:

Virtual Beings and Companions: AI can power virtual beings that inhabit the metaverse, offering companionship, guidance, and even entertainment. Imagine interacting with AI-powered characters that learn and evolve based on your interactions.

Personalized Experiences: AI can tailor metaverse experiences to individual preferences, generating personalized content, recommending activities, and even creating unique virtual environments based on your interests.

Interactive Storytelling: AI can create dynamic and interactive narratives within the metaverse, allowing users to participate in immersive stories, influence plotlines, and even create their own content.

The Ethical Considerations of AI in Entertainment

As AI becomes more deeply integrated into entertainment, it's crucial to address ethical considerations:

Job Displacement: The automation potential of AI raises concerns about job displacement in the entertainment industry. It's important to find ways to integrate AI responsibly, ensuring that it complements human creativity rather than replacing it entirely.

Bias and Representation: AI models are trained on data that may reflect existing biases in society. It's crucial to address these biases to ensure fair representation and avoid perpetuating harmful stereotypes in entertainment content.

Authenticity and Originality: As AI generates increasingly sophisticated content, questions arise about authorship, originality, and the value of human creativity. It's important to establish clear guidelines and ethical frameworks for AI-generated content.

The Future is Interactive and Intelligent

The future of entertainment is interactive, intelligent, and personalized, driven by the power of AI. LLaMA, with its language generation capabilities and open-source nature, is poised to play a key role in this transformation.

By embracing AI responsibly and fostering collaboration between human creativity and machine intelligence, we can unlock a new era of entertainment that is more engaging, immersive, and personalized than ever before. The future of entertainment is bright, and AI is illuminating the path forward.

Chapter 5

LLaMA in the Workplace

5.1 Automating Tasks: Boosting Productivity with AI

The modern workplace is a whirlwind of tasks, deadlines, and information overload. But what if we could offload some of the repetitive, time-consuming tasks to intelligent machines, freeing ourselves to focus on more strategic and creative endeavors? This chapter explores how AI, and specifically LLaMA, is automating tasks across various industries, boosting productivity, and reshaping the future of work.

The Rise of Intelligent Automation

Automation is not a new concept. From assembly lines to spreadsheets, we've long sought ways to streamline processes and increase efficiency. But AI is taking automation to a new level, enabling machines to perform tasks that once required human intelligence.

This "intelligent automation" is powered by technologies like machine learning, natural language processing, and computer vision, allowing machines to learn from data, understand human language, and even interpret visual information. This opens up a vast array of tasks that can be automated, from scheduling meetings and answering emails to analyzing data and generating reports.

LLaMA: The Automation Engine

LLaMA, with its language processing prowess, is particularly well-suited for automating tasks that involve text and communication. Here are some examples of how LLaMA can boost productivity:

Email Management: Imagine an AI assistant that can sort through your inbox, prioritize emails, and even generate responses to routine inquiries. LLaMA can analyze the content of your emails, understand your communication style, and craft personalized responses, saving you time and mental energy.

Meeting Scheduling: Scheduling meetings can be a tedious back-and-forth. LLaMA can automate this process, coordinating schedules, sending invitations, and even generating agendas based on the meeting's purpose.

Document Processing: Dealing with mountains of paperwork? LLaMA can analyze documents, extract key information, and even generate summaries, freeing you from tedious manual review.

Content Creation: LLaMA can generate various types of content, from social media posts and blog articles to reports and presentations. This allows you to focus on refining and editing the content, rather than starting from scratch.

Beyond the Office: AI Automation Across Industries

The impact of AI automation extends far beyond the office. Here are some examples of how LLaMA is being used in various industries:

Customer Service: AI-powered chatbots can handle customer inquiries, resolve issues, and provide 24/7 support, freeing up human agents to focus on more complex cases.

Healthcare: AI can automate administrative tasks, analyze medical records, and even assist in diagnosis, allowing healthcare professionals to focus on patient care.

Manufacturing: AI can optimize production processes, predict equipment failures, and even control robots on the assembly line, increasing efficiency and reducing costs.

Logistics: AI can optimize delivery routes, track shipments, and even predict potential delays, improving supply chain efficiency and customer satisfaction.

The Impact on the Workforce

The rise of AI automation raises important questions about the future of work. While some fear job displacement, others see an opportunity for humans and machines to collaborate, creating a more productive and fulfilling work environment.

AI automation can free humans from repetitive and mundane tasks, allowing them to focus on more creative, strategic, and interpersonal aspects of their work. This can lead to increased job satisfaction, improved work-life balance, and even the creation of new jobs in fields like AI development and maintenance.

The Future of AI Automation

The future of AI automation is bright, with continued advancements in AI technology promising even more sophisticated and impactful applications. LLaMA, with its open-source nature and focus on research, is poised to play a key role in shaping this future.

As AI automation becomes more prevalent, it's crucial to address ethical considerations, ensure responsible use, and foster a collaborative approach between humans and machines. By embracing AI as a tool for empowerment and productivity, we can create a future where work is more meaningful, fulfilling, and impactful.

5.2 Customer Service Revolution: LLaMA-Powered Chatbots

The days of frustrating phone menus, long wait times, and impersonal customer service interactions are fading fast. A new era of customer support is dawning, powered by artificial intelligence and fueled by the conversational prowess of large language models like LLaMA. This chapter explores how LLaMA-powered chatbots are revolutionizing customer service, creating more efficient, personalized, and satisfying experiences for both businesses and customers.

The Rise of the AI-Powered Assistant

Imagine contacting a company and being greeted by a friendly, helpful assistant who understands your needs, answers your questions accurately, and resolves your issues promptly. This is the promise of AI-powered chatbots.

These intelligent virtual assistants are trained on vast amounts of data, allowing them to understand natural language, identify customer intent, and provide relevant information or solutions. They can handle a wide range of tasks, from answering frequently asked questions to troubleshooting technical issues and even processing orders.

LLaMA, with its advanced language capabilities, is particularly well-suited for powering these chatbots. Its ability to generate human-quality text, understand context, and engage in natural-sounding conversations makes it an ideal tool for creating customer service experiences that are both efficient and empathetic.

Benefits for Businesses

LLaMA-powered chatbots offer numerous benefits for businesses:

24/7 Availability: Chatbots can provide round-the-clock support, ensuring that customers can get help whenever they need it, regardless of time zones or business hours.

Increased Efficiency: Chatbots can handle a large volume of inquiries simultaneously, freeing up human agents to focus on more complex or sensitive issues.

Cost Savings: By automating routine tasks, chatbots can reduce the need for large customer service teams, leading to significant cost savings.

Improved Customer Satisfaction: Chatbots can provide quick and accurate responses, resolving issues promptly and improving overall customer satisfaction.

Personalized Experiences: LLaMA's ability to understand context and generate personalized responses allows chatbots to tailor interactions to individual customer needs, creating a more engaging and satisfying experience.

Benefits for Customers

LLaMA-powered chatbots also offer significant advantages for customers:

Instant Support: No more waiting on hold or navigating complex phone menus. Chatbots provide instant access to assistance, resolving issues quickly and efficiently.

Personalized Service: Chatbots can remember past interactions, understand customer preferences, and provide tailored solutions, creating a more personalized and satisfying experience.

Convenience: Customers can interact with chatbots through various channels, including websites, messaging apps, and social media platforms, making it convenient to get help whenever and wherever they need it.

24/7 Availability: Customers can access support at any time, day or night, ensuring that their issues are addressed promptly, regardless of business hours.

Beyond Basic Support: LLaMA's Advanced Capabilities

LLaMA's advanced language capabilities enable chatbots to go beyond basic support, offering more sophisticated and personalized interactions:

Proactive Assistance: LLaMA-powered chatbots can anticipate customer needs and offer proactive assistance, such as suggesting relevant products or services or providing helpful information based on browsing history.

Emotional Intelligence: LLaMA can be trained to recognize and respond to emotions in customer language, allowing chatbots to provide empathetic support and build rapport with customers.

Multilingual Support: LLaMA's multilingual capabilities allow chatbots to communicate with customers in their preferred language, breaking down language barriers and expanding global reach.

The Future of Customer Service

LLaMA-powered chatbots are transforming the customer service landscape, creating more efficient, personalized, and satisfying experiences for both businesses and customers. As AI technology continues to evolve, we can expect even more sophisticated and human-like interactions, blurring the lines between human and machine and ushering in a new era of customer-centric support.

The future of customer service is intelligent, empathetic, and always available, thanks to the power of AI and the conversational prowess of LLaMA.

5.3 The Changing Job Market: Adapting to an AI-Driven World

The rise of artificial intelligence is transforming the job market in profound ways, creating both exciting opportunities and unprecedented challenges. This chapter explores the evolving landscape of work, examining how AI is reshaping industries, the skills needed to thrive in this new era, and the importance of adapting to an AI-driven world.

The Automation Revolution

AI is automating tasks across various sectors, from manufacturing and logistics to customer service and finance. This automation revolution is increasing efficiency, reducing costs, and changing the nature of many jobs.

Repetitive tasks: AI excels at automating repetitive, rule-based tasks, such as data entry, document processing, and even some aspects of customer support. This frees up human workers to focus on more complex and creative endeavors.

Data analysis: AI algorithms can analyze vast amounts of data, identifying patterns and insights that would be impossible for humans to discern. This is transforming fields like finance, marketing, and healthcare, where data-driven decision-making is crucial.

Physical tasks: Robots powered by AI are increasingly taking over physical tasks in manufacturing, logistics, and even surgery. This improves precision, reduces errors, and enhances safety in these industries.

The Rise of New Jobs

While AI is automating some jobs, it's also creating new opportunities. The development, implementation, and maintenance of AI systems require a skilled workforce.

AI specialists: Demand for AI specialists, including data scientists, machine learning engineers, and AI ethicists, is skyrocketing. These professionals develop and refine AI algorithms, ensuring their responsible and ethical implementation.

Human-AI collaboration: Many jobs will involve collaborating with AI systems. This requires workers to understand how AI works, interpret its outputs, and leverage its capabilities to enhance their own productivity.

Creativity and critical thinking: As AI takes over routine tasks, human skills like creativity, critical thinking, and problem-solving become even more valuable. These skills are essential for navigating complex situations, developing innovative solutions, and adapting to the changing demands of the workplace.

Adapting to the AI-Driven World

Thriving in the AI-driven job market requires adaptability, continuous learning, and a focus on developing essential skills:

Digital literacy: A strong foundation in digital technologies is crucial. This includes understanding basic computer skills, navigating digital tools, and adapting to new technologies as they emerge.

Data literacy: The ability to understand, interpret, and work with data is increasingly important. This involves skills like data analysis, visualization, and critical thinking.

Critical thinking and problem-solving: AI can provide solutions, but humans are needed to interpret those solutions, identify potential biases, and apply critical thinking to make informed decisions.

Creativity and innovation: AI can automate routine tasks, but human creativity is essential for developing new ideas, solving complex problems, and driving innovation.

Communication and collaboration: Working with AI often involves collaborating with both humans and machines. Strong communication and interpersonal skills are crucial for effective teamwork in this environment.

Embracing Lifelong Learning

The rapid pace of technological change means that lifelong learning is no longer optional; it's essential for staying relevant in the AI-driven job market.

Upskilling and reskilling: Workers need to continuously update their skills and knowledge to adapt to the changing demands of the workplace. This may involve acquiring new technical skills, developing AI literacy, or focusing on uniquely human skills like creativity and critical thinking.

Embracing change: The ability to embrace change and adapt to new technologies is crucial. This involves a growth mindset, a willingness to learn, and a proactive approach to professional development.

The Future of Work

The AI-driven job market presents both challenges and opportunities. By adapting to the changing landscape, developing essential skills, and embracing lifelong learning, individuals can thrive in this new era of work.

The future of work is not about humans vs. machines; it's about humans and machines working together to achieve greater productivity, innovation, and fulfillment. By embracing AI as a tool for empowerment and collaboration, we can create a future where work is more meaningful, engaging, and rewarding for all.

Chapter 6

LLaMA and Scientific Discovery

6.1 Accelerating Research: Analyzing Data and Generating Hypotheses

The lifeblood of scientific discovery is data. It's the raw material from which we extract knowledge, build theories, and push the boundaries of understanding. But the sheer volume of data generated in modern research can be overwhelming, leaving scientists struggling to sift through the noise and extract meaningful insights. This is where AI steps in, offering a powerful new set of tools to accelerate research, analyze data with unprecedented speed and accuracy, and even generate novel hypotheses that could lead to groundbreaking discoveries.

LLaMA: A Data Scientist's Ally

LLaMA, with its ability to process and analyze vast amounts of text, is a game-changer for data-driven research. It can sift through research papers, extract key findings, identify trends, and even uncover hidden connections that might otherwise go unnoticed. This allows scientists to:

Stay Ahead of the Curve: LLaMA can keep researchers up-to-date on the latest findings in their field, even across rapidly evolving disciplines. Imagine having an AI assistant that constantly scans new publications, summarizes key findings, and alerts you to relevant research.

Uncover Hidden Connections: By analyzing vast datasets, LLaMA can identify patterns and correlations that might be missed by human researchers. This can lead to new insights, spark novel research questions, and even reveal unexpected connections between seemingly disparate fields.

Accelerate Literature Reviews: LLaMA can automate the tedious process of literature review, summarizing key findings from multiple studies, identifying contradictory results, and highlighting areas where further research is needed.

From Data to Hypothesis: LLaMA's Inductive Leap

LLaMA doesn't just analyze data; it can also generate hypotheses. By identifying patterns and trends in existing data, LLaMA can propose new research questions, suggest potential explanations, and even formulate testable hypotheses. This can be a powerful tool for:

Exploring New Territories: LLaMA can help researchers explore uncharted territories by generating hypotheses that challenge existing assumptions and push the boundaries of scientific inquiry.

Overcoming Bias: Human researchers can be influenced by their own biases and preconceptions. LLaMA, with its objective approach to data analysis, can help overcome these biases and generate hypotheses that might not have occurred to human researchers.

Sparking Creativity: LLaMA can act as a creative spark, generating unexpected hypotheses that challenge conventional thinking and lead to novel research directions.

Applications Across Scientific Domains

The potential of LLaMA to accelerate research and generate hypotheses extends across various scientific domains:

Drug Discovery: LLaMA can analyze vast databases of chemical compounds, predict their potential interactions with biological targets, and even suggest novel drug candidates. This can significantly accelerate the drug discovery process, leading to the development of new treatments for diseases.

Genomics: LLaMA can analyze genomic data, identify genetic mutations associated with diseases, and even predict the risk of developing certain conditions. This can contribute to personalized medicine, allowing for tailored treatments and preventative measures based on individual genetic profiles.

Materials Science: LLaMA can analyze the properties of different materials, predict their behavior under various conditions, and even suggest new materials with specific characteristics. This can accelerate the development of new materials for applications in energy, construction, and other industries.

Environmental Science: LLaMA can analyze environmental data, model climate patterns, and predict the impact of environmental changes on various ecosystems. This can help us understand the complex dynamics of our planet and develop strategies to mitigate the effects of climate change.

The Future of AI-Driven Research

As AI technology continues to evolve, we can expect even more sophisticated tools and applications to emerge in the realm of scientific research. LLaMA, with its open-source nature and focus on research, is poised to play a key role in shaping this future.

Imagine a world where scientists can seamlessly collaborate with AI partners, where data analysis is automated, and where new discoveries are accelerated by the intelligence of machines. This is the future of AI-driven research, a future where human curiosity and machine intelligence converge to unlock the mysteries of the universe and drive progress for the benefit of humankind.

6.2 Drug Discovery and Development: LLaMA's Role in Healthcare

The quest to conquer disease and improve human health has always been a driving force in scientific innovation. But the traditional process of drug discovery and development is often a long, complex, and costly journey, riddled with setbacks and dead ends. Now, artificial intelligence is emerging as a powerful ally in this quest, offering new tools and approaches to accelerate the development of life-saving treatments. This chapter explores the exciting role of LLaMA in revolutionizing drug discovery and development, paving the way for a healthier future.

Accelerating the Search for New Medicines

The traditional drug discovery process involves identifying promising drug candidates, testing their efficacy and safety in preclinical studies, and then conducting clinical trials in humans. This process can take years, even decades, and often faces high failure rates.

LLaMA, with its ability to analyze vast amounts of data and generate novel hypotheses, can significantly accelerate this process:

Target Identification: LLaMA can analyze scientific literature, genomic data, and clinical trial results to identify promising drug targets – the specific molecules or pathways involved in disease processes.

Drug Candidate Generation: LLaMA can analyze the properties of various chemical compounds, predict their potential interactions with drug targets, and even generate novel drug candidates with desired characteristics. This can significantly expand the pool of potential drugs and increase the chances of finding effective treatments.

Preclinical Studies: LLaMA can analyze preclinical data, predict the efficacy and safety of drug candidates, and even suggest optimal dosages and treatment regimens. This can help prioritize promising candidates and reduce the risk of failures in later stages of development.

Optimizing Clinical Trials

Clinical trials are a crucial step in drug development, but they can be time-consuming, expensive, and challenging to conduct. LLaMA can help optimize clinical trials in several ways:

Patient Selection: LLaMA can analyze patient data to identify individuals who are most likely to benefit from a particular treatment. This can improve the efficiency of clinical trials and increase the chances of success.

Predicting Treatment Response: LLaMA can analyze patient data and predict their response to different treatments. This can help personalize treatment plans and improve patient outcomes.

Monitoring Safety and Efficacy: LLaMA can analyze clinical trial data to monitor the safety and efficacy of new drugs, identify potential side effects, and even predict the long-term outcomes of treatment.

Personalized Medicine: Tailoring Treatments to Individuals

LLaMA's ability to analyze individual patient data opens up exciting possibilities for personalized medicine, where treatments are tailored to each patient's unique needs and genetic makeup.

Predicting Disease Risk: LLaMA can analyze genomic data and lifestyle factors to predict an individual's risk of developing certain diseases. This can enable preventative measures and early interventions.

Personalized Treatment Plans: LLaMA can analyze patient data to predict their response to different treatments, allowing for personalized treatment plans that optimize efficacy and minimize side effects.

Drug Repurposing: LLaMA can identify existing drugs that could be repurposed for new indications, potentially accelerating the development of treatments for rare or neglected diseases.

The Future of AI in Healthcare

The applications of LLaMA in healthcare extend beyond drug discovery and development. It can also be used for:

Medical Diagnosis: LLaMA can analyze medical images, such as X-rays and MRIs, to assist in diagnosis and identify potential abnormalities.

Patient Education: LLaMA can generate personalized educational materials for patients, explaining their conditions, treatment options, and potential side effects in clear and understandable language.

Mental Health Support: LLaMA can power chatbots that provide mental health support, offering a listening ear, providing coping strategies, and even connecting individuals with mental health professionals.

The Ethical Considerations of AI in Healthcare

As AI becomes more integrated into healthcare, it's crucial to address ethical considerations:

Data Privacy and Security: Protecting patient data is paramount. AI systems must be designed with robust security measures to ensure patient privacy and prevent data breaches.

Bias and Fairness: AI models must be trained on diverse and representative datasets to avoid biases that could lead to unequal access to healthcare or discriminatory treatment.

Transparency and Explainability: AI systems used in healthcare should be transparent and explainable, allowing healthcare professionals to understand how they arrive at their recommendations and make informed decisions.

A Healthier Future with AI

LLaMA and other AI technologies are transforming healthcare, offering new tools and approaches to accelerate drug discovery, optimize clinical trials, and personalize treatments. By embracing AI responsibly and addressing ethical considerations, we can create a future where healthcare is more efficient, effective, and accessible for all.

The future of healthcare is intelligent, personalized, and driven by the power of AI. LLaMA is playing a key role in this transformation, paving the way for a healthier future for humankind.

6.3 Environmental Applications: Using AI for Sustainability

Our planet faces unprecedented environmental challenges, from climate change and pollution to deforestation and resource depletion. Tackling these challenges requires innovative solutions and a global commitment to sustainability. Artificial intelligence, with its ability to analyze complex data, predict environmental changes, and optimize resource management, is emerging as a powerful tool in the fight for a greener future. This chapter explores the diverse environmental applications of AI, highlighting how it can be used to protect our planet and create a more sustainable world.

Monitoring and Predicting Environmental Changes

AI can analyze vast amounts of environmental data from various sources, including satellites, sensors, and weather stations, to monitor and predict environmental changes. This enables:

Climate Modeling: AI can analyze climate data to model climate patterns, predict future changes, and assess the impact of climate change on various ecosystems. This information can inform policy decisions and guide mitigation efforts.

Pollution Monitoring: AI can analyze air and water quality data to monitor pollution levels, identify sources of pollution, and predict potential environmental hazards. This can help authorities take proactive measures to protect public health and the environment.

Deforestation Detection: AI can analyze satellite imagery to detect deforestation in real-time, allowing for rapid response and prevention of illegal logging activities.

Biodiversity Monitoring: AI can analyze images and sounds from wildlife cameras and sensors to identify and track endangered species, monitor their populations, and assess the health of ecosystems.

Optimizing Resource Management

AI can optimize the use of natural resources, reducing waste and promoting sustainability. This includes:

Precision Agriculture: AI can analyze soil data, weather patterns, and crop health to optimize irrigation, fertilization, and pest control, reducing the environmental impact of agriculture and improving crop yields.

Water Management: AI can optimize water distribution, predict water demand, and detect leaks in water infrastructure, ensuring efficient use of this precious resource.

Energy Efficiency: AI can optimize energy consumption in buildings and industrial processes, reducing energy waste and greenhouse gas emissions.

Waste Management: AI can analyze waste streams, optimize recycling processes, and identify opportunities for waste reduction, minimizing the environmental impact of waste disposal.

Developing Sustainable Solutions

AI can contribute to the development of sustainable solutions in various sectors:

Renewable Energy: AI can optimize the design and operation of renewable energy systems, such as solar and wind farms, improving their efficiency and reliability.

Sustainable Transportation: AI can optimize traffic flow, reduce congestion, and promote the use of electric vehicles, reducing greenhouse gas emissions from transportation.

Green Buildings: AI can optimize building design and operation to minimize energy consumption, reduce water usage, and improve indoor environmental quality.

Sustainable Manufacturing: AI can optimize manufacturing processes to reduce waste, minimize energy consumption, and promote the use of sustainable materials.

Empowering Citizen Science

AI can empower citizen scientists to contribute to environmental monitoring and conservation efforts. This includes:

Species Identification: AI-powered apps can help citizens identify and report sightings of different species, contributing to biodiversity monitoring and conservation efforts.

Pollution Reporting: Citizens can use AI-powered apps to report pollution incidents, providing valuable data for environmental monitoring and enforcement.

Environmental Awareness: AI can personalize environmental information and recommendations, encouraging individuals to adopt sustainable practices in their daily lives.

The Future of AI for Sustainability

AI is poised to play an increasingly important role in addressing environmental challenges and creating a more sustainable future. As AI technology continues to evolve, we can expect even more innovative and impactful applications in the realm of environmental sustainability.

The future of AI for sustainability involves:

Enhanced Prediction and Modeling: AI will become even more sophisticated in predicting environmental changes and modeling complex environmental systems.

Increased Automation: AI will automate more tasks in environmental monitoring, resource management, and sustainable development.

Greater Personalization: AI will provide personalized environmental information and recommendations, empowering individuals to make sustainable choices.

Enhanced Collaboration: AI will facilitate collaboration between scientists, policymakers, and citizens in addressing environmental challenges.

By harnessing the power of AI responsibly and ethically, we can create a future where technology and nature coexist in harmony, ensuring a healthy and sustainable planet for generations to come.

Chapter 7

The Ethics of LLaMA

7.1 Bias and Fairness: Addressing Concerns in AI

Artificial intelligence holds immense promise for improving our lives and solving complex challenges. However, as AI systems become more prevalent, it's crucial to address concerns about bias and fairness. This chapter delves into the issue of bias in AI, exploring its sources, its potential consequences, and the strategies being developed to mitigate its impact and ensure fairness in AI applications.

Understanding Bias in AI

Bias in AI arises when an AI system produces outcomes that are systematically prejudiced due to flawed assumptions in the machine learning algorithms or the data used to train them. This can lead to AI systems that unfairly favor or discriminate against certain groups based on factors like race, gender, age, or socioeconomic status.

Sources of Bias

Bias in AI can stem from various sources:

Biased Data: AI models learn from the data they are trained on. If the training data reflects existing biases in society, the AI system will likely perpetuate those biases in its outputs. For example, if a facial recognition system is trained primarily on images of light-skinned individuals, it may perform poorly on images of people with darker skin tones.

Algorithmic Bias: The algorithms themselves can also introduce bias. If the algorithm is designed with flawed assumptions or prioritizes certain features over others, it can lead to biased outcomes.

Human Bias: Even with unbiased data and algorithms, human biases can creep into AI systems. The choices made by developers in designing, training, and deploying AI systems can reflect their own biases, consciously or unconsciously.

Potential Consequences of Bias

Bias in AI can have serious consequences, including:

Discrimination: Biased AI systems can perpetuate and even amplify existing societal biases, leading to discrimination in areas like hiring, lending, criminal justice, and healthcare.

Inequity: Biased AI can create or exacerbate inequalities, denying opportunities or resources to certain groups based on their protected characteristics.

Erosion of Trust: If people perceive AI systems as unfair or biased, it can erode trust in these technologies, hindering their adoption and limiting their potential benefits.

Mitigating Bias and Ensuring Fairness

Addressing bias in AI requires a multi-faceted approach:

Diverse and Representative Data: AI models should be trained on diverse and representative datasets that reflect the full spectrum of human characteristics and experiences. This can help reduce the risk of perpetuating existing biases.

Fairness-Aware Algorithms: Researchers are developing algorithms that are explicitly designed to be fairness-aware, taking into account potential biases and mitigating their impact on outcomes.

Transparency and Explainability: AI systems should be transparent and explainable, allowing humans to understand how they work and identify potential biases.

Human Oversight and Accountability: Human oversight is crucial in ensuring fairness in AI applications. This involves establishing clear ethical guidelines, providing training on bias awareness, and holding developers and deployers accountable for the outcomes of their AI systems.

Continuous Monitoring and Evaluation: AI systems should be continuously monitored and evaluated for bias, with mechanisms in place to address any biases that emerge over time.

LLaMA and Fairness

LLaMA, with its open-source nature and focus on research, has the potential to contribute to the development of fairer AI systems. Its transparency allows researchers to examine its inner workings and identify potential biases. Its open-source nature encourages community involvement in identifying and addressing biases.

However, LLaMA, like any LLM, is susceptible to bias if trained on biased data. It's crucial to ensure that the data used to train LLaMA is diverse, representative, and free from harmful biases.

The Path to Fairer AI

Creating fair and unbiased AI systems is an ongoing challenge, but it's a crucial one to address. By acknowledging the potential for bias, developing mitigation strategies, and fostering a culture of fairness and accountability, we can harness the power of AI for the benefit of all, ensuring that these technologies promote equity and justice rather than perpetuating harmful biases.

7.2 Privacy and Security: Protecting Data in the Age of LLaMA

The rise of powerful AI models like LLaMA brings with it a critical responsibility: protecting privacy and ensuring data security. This chapter explores the unique challenges and opportunities presented by LLaMA in the realm of data protection, outlining best practices and ethical considerations for responsible AI development and deployment.

The Data Dilemma: Power and Responsibility

LLaMA, like other large language models, is trained on massive datasets of text and code. This data fuels its ability to understand and generate human language, but it also raises concerns about privacy and security.

Sensitive Information: Training data can contain sensitive personal information, such as names, addresses, phone numbers, and even private conversations. If this information is not properly anonymized or protected, it could be inadvertently revealed or misused.

Data Breaches: Large datasets are attractive targets for cyberattacks. A data breach could expose sensitive information, leading to identity theft, financial loss, or even reputational damage.

Misuse of Data: Even if data is anonymized, it could be misused to create targeted advertising, manipulate public opinion, or even generate deepfakes.

Protecting Privacy in the Age of LLaMA

Protecting privacy in the age of LLaMA requires a multi-faceted approach:

Data Minimization: Collect and use only the data that is absolutely necessary for training and deploying LLaMA. Avoid collecting sensitive information whenever possible.

Data Anonymization: Remove any personally identifiable information from training data. This can involve techniques like pseudonymization, where identifying information is replaced with pseudonyms, or differential privacy, which adds noise to data to protect individual privacy.

Secure Data Storage: Store data securely, using encryption and access controls to prevent unauthorized access. Implement robust cybersecurity measures to protect against data breaches.

Transparency and Control: Be transparent about how data is collected, used, and stored. Provide users with control over their data, allowing them to access, correct, or delete their information.

Differential Privacy: Implement differential privacy techniques to add noise to data and protect individual privacy while still allowing for meaningful analysis.

Federated Learning: Explore federated learning techniques, where models are trained on decentralized data sources without directly accessing the data itself. This can help protect privacy while still allowing for collaborative model development.

LLaMA's Open-Source Advantage

LLaMA's open-source nature can contribute to enhanced privacy and security in several ways:

Transparency: The open-source nature of LLaMA allows researchers and developers to scrutinize its code, identify potential privacy vulnerabilities, and contribute to solutions.

Community Oversight: The open-source community can act as a watchdog, holding developers accountable for privacy and security practices.

Collaboration: Open-source collaboration can foster the development of privacy-enhancing technologies and best practices for responsible AI development.

Ethical Considerations

Beyond technical measures, protecting privacy and security in the age of LLaMA requires ethical considerations:

Respect for User Privacy: Prioritize user privacy in the design, development, and deployment of LLaMA applications. Obtain informed consent for data collection and use.

Responsible Data Handling: Handle data responsibly, ensuring its accuracy, completeness, and security. Avoid using data for purposes that are not explicitly disclosed to users.

Accountability: Establish clear lines of accountability for data privacy and security. Implement mechanisms for addressing privacy breaches and data misuse.

The Future of Privacy and AI

As AI technology continues to evolve, the challenges and opportunities related to privacy and security will also evolve. Staying ahead of these challenges requires ongoing research, collaboration, and a commitment to ethical AI development.

The future of privacy and AI involves:

Developing Privacy-Preserving AI Techniques: Researchers are actively developing new techniques to train and deploy AI models while protecting privacy. This includes techniques like federated learning, differential privacy, and homomorphic encryption.

Strengthening Regulatory Frameworks: Governments and regulatory bodies are working to establish clear guidelines and regulations for AI development and deployment, with a focus on protecting privacy and ensuring ethical use.

Promoting Ethical AI Practices: The AI community is increasingly focused on promoting ethical AI practices, including responsible data handling, transparency, and accountability.

By embracing these principles and prioritizing privacy and security in the development and deployment of LLaMA, we can harness the power of AI while safeguarding sensitive information and building trust in these transformative technologies.

7.3 Responsible AI Development: Meta's Approach

Meta, the company behind LLaMA, recognizes the immense power of AI and the responsibility that comes with it. This chapter delves into Meta's approach to responsible AI development, examining its core principles, its initiatives, and its commitment to building AI that benefits humanity while mitigating potential risks.

Meta's Five Pillars of Responsible AI

Meta's approach to responsible AI is grounded in five core pillars:

1 Privacy and Security: Protecting the privacy and security of people's data is paramount. Meta implements robust data security measures, anonymizes data whenever possible, and provides users with control over their information.

2 Fairness: AI systems should treat everyone fairly and avoid perpetuating biases. Meta invests in research to mitigate bias, promotes fairness in its algorithms, and strives to create inclusive AI experiences.

3 Safety and Integrity: AI systems should be safe, reliable, and behave as intended. Meta conducts rigorous testing, implements safeguards, and monitors its AI systems for potential harms.

4 Transparency and Control: People should have transparency into how AI systems work and have control over their interactions with AI. Meta provides information about its AI systems, explains how they make decisions, and offers users choices in how they interact with AI.

5 Accountability: Meta is accountable for the responsible development and use of its AI systems. It establishes clear ethical guidelines, provides training on responsible AI practices, and engages with the broader community to address concerns and ensure accountability.

Initiatives and Practices

Meta is actively implementing various initiatives and practices to uphold its responsible AI principles:

Responsible AI Research: Meta invests in research to address key challenges in responsible AI, such as bias detection, fairness-aware algorithms, and explainable AI.

Collaboration and Partnerships: Meta collaborates with academic institutions, industry partners, and civil society organizations to advance responsible AI development and address ethical concerns.

Open Source and Community Engagement: Meta embraces open-source principles, making some of its AI models and tools available to the research community. This fosters transparency, collaboration, and community-driven innovation in responsible AI.

Ethical Review Process: Meta has established an ethical review process for its AI systems, involving experts from various disciplines to assess potential risks and ensure alignment with ethical principles.

AI Red Teaming: Meta employs AI red teaming techniques, where internal and external experts try to find vulnerabilities or potential harms in AI systems before they are deployed.

Bias Bounties: Meta offers "bias bounties" to encourage researchers and the public to identify and report biases in its AI systems.

Transparency Tools: Meta develops tools to provide transparency into its AI systems, such as "Why am I seeing this?" explanations for content recommendations.

Addressing the Challenges of Generative AI

Meta recognizes that generative AI models, like LLaMA, present unique challenges in responsible AI development. These models can generate highly realistic and convincing content, which raises concerns about potential misuse, such as creating deepfakes or spreading misinformation.

Meta is taking steps to address these challenges:

Safety Mechanisms: Meta is developing safety mechanisms to prevent the generation of harmful or misleading content, such as filtering out toxic language or detecting deepfakes.

Content Policies: Meta has established clear content policies that prohibit the use of its AI systems for malicious purposes.

Education and Awareness: Meta is educating users about the capabilities and limitations of generative AI and raising awareness about potential risks.

Ongoing Commitment

Meta's commitment to responsible AI development is an ongoing journey. The company recognizes that the field of AI is constantly evolving, and new challenges and opportunities will emerge. Meta is dedicated to continuous learning, adaptation, and collaboration to ensure that its AI systems are developed and used responsibly, ethically, and for the benefit of humanity.

By upholding its five pillars of responsible AI, investing in research and development, and engaging with the broader community, Meta is striving to be a leader in responsible AI innovation, creating AI that empowers individuals, strengthens communities, and contributes to a better future for all.

Chapter 8

LLaMA and Society

8.1 The Impact on Education: Learning with AI

The classroom of the future is no longer a futuristic fantasy; it's being shaped by the rapid advancements in artificial intelligence. AI is poised to revolutionize education, personalizing the learning experience, enhancing accessibility, and empowering both students and educators. This chapter explores the transformative impact of AI on education, highlighting its potential to create a more engaging, effective, and inclusive learning environment for all.

Personalized Learning: Tailoring Education to Individual Needs

Imagine a learning experience that adapts to each student's unique needs, pace, and learning style. AI is making this a reality, enabling personalized learning at scale.

Adaptive Learning Platforms: AI-powered platforms can assess students' strengths and weaknesses, provide personalized feedback, and tailor learning pathways to individual needs. This ensures that students are challenged appropriately and receive the support they need to succeed.

AI Tutors: AI tutors can provide personalized guidance and support, answering questions, explaining concepts, and offering encouragement. These virtual tutors can be available 24/7, providing on-demand assistance whenever students need it.

Customized Learning Materials: AI can generate customized learning materials, such as practice exercises, quizzes, and study guides, tailored to individual student needs and preferences. This ensures that students are engaged with material that is relevant and challenging.

Enhancing Accessibility and Inclusion

AI can break down barriers to education, making learning more accessible and inclusive for all students:

Students with Disabilities: AI can provide personalized support for students with disabilities, such as generating text-to-speech and speech-to-text conversions, providing real-time captioning for videos, and even translating educational materials into different languages.

Remote Learning: AI can enhance remote learning experiences by providing personalized support, facilitating communication and collaboration, and creating engaging virtual learning environments.

Addressing Learning Gaps: AI can identify and address learning gaps, providing targeted interventions and support to help students catch up and succeed.

Empowering Educators

AI can empower educators by automating tasks, providing insights into student learning, and freeing up time for more meaningful interactions with students.

Automating Administrative Tasks: AI can automate tasks like grading assignments, providing feedback, and even generating lesson plans. This allows educators to focus on more interactive and personalized instruction.

Data-Driven Insights: AI can analyze student data to provide insights into learning patterns, identify areas where students are struggling, and inform instructional strategies.

Personalized Professional Development: AI can provide personalized professional development opportunities for educators, recommending resources, courses, and workshops based on their individual needs and goals.

Creating Engaging Learning Experiences

AI can make learning more engaging and interactive, sparking curiosity and fostering a love of learning.

Gamification: AI can be used to create educational games and simulations that make learning fun and engaging.

Interactive Content: AI can generate interactive learning materials, such as virtual field trips, simulations, and experiments, that allow students to explore concepts in a hands-on way.

Personalized Feedback: AI can provide personalized feedback that is specific, timely, and actionable, helping students understand their strengths and areas for improvement.

The Ethical Considerations of AI in Education

As AI becomes more integrated into education, it's crucial to address ethical considerations:

Data Privacy and Security: Protecting student data is paramount. AI systems must be designed with robust security measures to ensure student privacy and prevent data breaches.

Bias and Fairness: AI models must be trained on diverse and representative datasets to avoid biases that could perpetuate inequalities in education.

Transparency and Explainability: AI systems used in education should be transparent and explainable, allowing educators and students to understand how they work and make informed decisions.

Human-Centered Design: AI should be used to enhance, not replace, human interaction in education. The focus should be on creating AI tools that empower both students and educators.

The Future of Learning with AI

AI is transforming education, creating a future where learning is personalized, accessible, and engaging for all. As AI technology continues to evolve, we can expect even more innovative and impactful applications in the realm of education.

The future of learning with AI involves:

Lifelong Learning: AI will support lifelong learning, providing personalized learning opportunities and resources for individuals of all ages and backgrounds.

AI-Augmented Creativity: AI will foster creativity and innovation in education, empowering students to explore new ideas and express themselves in unique ways.

Global Collaboration: AI will facilitate global collaboration in education, connecting students and educators from around the world and fostering cross-cultural understanding.

By embracing AI responsibly and ethically, we can create a future where education empowers individuals, strengthens communities, and prepares future generations for the challenges and opportunities of an AI-driven world.

8.2 Social Connections: How LLaMA is Changing Communication

We live in an age of unprecedented interconnectedness, where communication technologies bridge continents and connect people in ways never before imagined. Yet, paradoxically, feelings of isolation and loneliness are also on the rise. This chapter explores how AI, and specifically LLaMA, is changing the landscape of social connection, offering new tools for communication, fostering understanding across cultures, and even combating social isolation.

Breaking Down Barriers: AI for Enhanced Communication

LLaMA, with its advanced language capabilities, can enhance communication in several ways:

Overcoming Language Barriers: LLaMA's multilingual capabilities can translate languages in real-time, facilitating cross-cultural communication and understanding. Imagine conversing effortlessly with someone who speaks a different language, with LLaMA seamlessly translating your words.

Accessibility: LLaMA can generate text-to-speech and speech-to-text conversions, making communication more accessible for people with disabilities. This can empower individuals who have difficulty speaking or hearing to connect with others more easily.

Personalized Communication: LLaMA can analyze communication styles and preferences, tailoring messages to individual needs and fostering more effective communication. This can help build stronger relationships and avoid misunderstandings.

Fostering Understanding and Empathy

LLaMA can be used to foster understanding and empathy by:

Analyzing Sentiment: LLaMA can analyze text and speech to identify emotional cues, helping people better understand the emotions and intentions behind communication. This can lead to more empathetic and productive conversations.

Generating Diverse Perspectives: LLaMA can generate different perspectives on a topic, encouraging open-mindedness and challenging biases. This can foster understanding and bridge divides between people with different viewpoints.

Facilitating Dialogue: LLaMA can be used to create chatbots that facilitate dialogue and encourage meaningful conversations. This can help people connect with others who share their interests or experiences, even if they are geographically separated.

Combating Social Isolation

Loneliness and social isolation are growing concerns in our increasingly digital world. LLaMA can be used to combat social isolation by:

Providing Companionship: LLaMA-powered chatbots can provide companionship and conversation for people who are lonely or isolated. These chatbots can engage in meaningful conversations, offer support, and even provide a sense of connection.

Connecting People with Shared Interests: LLaMA can connect people with shared interests, facilitating the formation of online communities and support groups. This can help people find others who understand their experiences and provide a sense of belonging.

Encouraging Social Interaction: LLaMA can be used to create interactive games and activities that encourage social interaction and communication. This can help people break out of their social isolation and connect with others in a fun and engaging way.

The Ethical Considerations of AI in Social Connection

As AI becomes more integrated into our social lives, it's important to address ethical considerations:

Authenticity and Deception: It's important to be transparent about when people are interacting with AI, avoiding deception and ensuring that users are aware of the capabilities and limitations of AI systems.

Privacy and Data Security: Protecting user data is crucial. AI systems used in social contexts must be designed with robust privacy and security measures to prevent data breaches and misuse of personal information.

Algorithmic Bias: AI models can perpetuate biases if they are trained on biased data. It's important to address these biases to ensure that AI systems promote fairness and inclusivity in social interactions.

The Future of Social Connection with AI

LLaMA and other AI technologies are changing how we connect, communicate, and build relationships. As AI continues to evolve, we can expect even more innovative and impactful applications in the realm of social connection.

The future of social connection with AI involves:

More Human-like Interactions: AI will become even more sophisticated in understanding and responding to human emotions, creating more natural and empathetic interactions.

Enhanced Accessibility: AI will continue to break down barriers to communication, making it easier for people with disabilities to connect and interact with others.

Personalized Connections: AI will personalize social experiences, connecting people with others who share their interests, values, and goals.

By embracing AI responsibly and ethically, we can create a future where technology enhances our social lives, fosters understanding, and combats social isolation, leading to a more connected and compassionate world.

8.3 The Digital Divide: Ensuring Equitable Access to AI

The transformative power of AI holds the potential to revolutionize industries, improve lives, and solve some of the world's most pressing challenges. However, the benefits of AI are not guaranteed to be distributed equally. This chapter examines the digital divide in the context of AI, exploring the factors that contribute to unequal access, the potential consequences of this divide, and the strategies needed to ensure equitable access to AI for all.

Understanding the Digital Divide in the Age of AI

The digital divide refers to the gap between those who have access to technology and those who do not. In the age of AI, this divide encompasses not only access to the internet and digital devices but also access to AI technologies, skills, and opportunities.

Factors Contributing to the AI Divide

Several factors contribute to the digital divide in the context of AI:

Socioeconomic Disparities: Individuals and communities with lower socioeconomic status often have limited access to the resources needed to participate in the AI revolution, such as high-speed internet, powerful computers, and educational opportunities.

Geographical Barriers: Access to AI technologies and infrastructure may be limited in rural or remote areas, creating a geographical divide in AI access and opportunities.

Educational Inequalities: Lack of access to quality education, particularly in STEM fields, can limit individuals' ability to develop the skills needed to participate in the AI workforce or leverage AI technologies effectively.

Digital Literacy: Even with access to technology, individuals may lack the digital literacy skills needed to navigate the digital world, use AI tools, and critically evaluate AI-generated information.

Bias and Discrimination: Bias in AI algorithms and datasets can perpetuate existing inequalities, denying opportunities or resources to certain groups based on their race, gender, or other protected characteristics.

Potential Consequences of the AI Divide

The AI divide can have significant consequences, including:

Exacerbated Inequality: Unequal access to AI can exacerbate existing social and economic inequalities, creating a widening gap between those who benefit from AI and those who are left behind.

Limited Opportunity: The AI divide can limit opportunities for individuals and communities, denying them access to education, employment, and other benefits of AI technologies.

Social Exclusion: Those without access to AI may be excluded from participating fully in an increasingly AI-driven society, leading to social isolation and marginalization.

Reduced Innovation: A lack of diversity in the AI workforce can limit innovation and creativity, as diverse perspectives and experiences are crucial for developing AI solutions that benefit everyone.

Bridging the AI Divide: Strategies for Equitable Access

Ensuring equitable access to AI requires a multi-faceted approach:

Investing in Infrastructure: Expanding access to affordable high-speed internet and digital devices is crucial, particularly in underserved communities.

Promoting Digital Literacy: Providing education and training on digital literacy, AI concepts, and ethical considerations is essential for empowering individuals to participate in the AI era.

Supporting STEM Education: Investing in quality STEM education, from early childhood through higher education, can equip individuals with the skills needed to thrive in an AI-driven world.

Addressing Bias and Discrimination: Developing fairness-aware algorithms, promoting diversity in the AI workforce, and implementing ethical guidelines can help mitigate bias and ensure equitable outcomes.

Fostering Inclusive Innovation: Creating opportunities for individuals from diverse backgrounds to participate in AI development and innovation can lead to more inclusive and beneficial AI solutions.

Community-Driven Initiatives: Supporting community-driven initiatives that provide access to AI education, resources, and opportunities can empower local communities to bridge the AI divide.

LLaMA and Equitable Access

LLaMA, with its open-source nature and focus on research, has the potential to contribute to bridging the AI divide. Its accessibility allows researchers, developers, and educators from diverse backgrounds to experiment with and build upon the model, fostering a more inclusive AI ecosystem.

However, it's crucial to ensure that LLaMA is developed and deployed responsibly, with a focus on fairness, transparency, and ethical considerations. This includes addressing potential biases in the model and ensuring that its applications benefit all members of society.

A Shared Responsibility

Bridging the AI divide is a shared responsibility that requires collaboration between governments, businesses, educational institutions, and community organizations. By working together, we can ensure that the benefits of AI are accessible to all, creating a more equitable and inclusive future for everyone in the age of AI.

Chapter 9

The Future of LLaMA

9.1 Advancements in Development: What's Next for Meta's AI

Meta's AI journey is far from over. The company continues to push the boundaries of AI research and development, exploring new frontiers and expanding the capabilities of its AI systems. This chapter delves into the exciting advancements on the horizon for Meta's AI, examining the key areas of focus and the potential impact of these innovations.

Enhanced Language Understanding and Generation

Meta is constantly working to improve the language understanding and generation capabilities of its AI models, including LLaMA. This involves:

Larger and More Powerful Models: Meta is exploring the development of even larger and more powerful language models, with increased capacity for learning and generating more nuanced and complex language.

Multimodal AI: Meta is integrating different modalities, such as images, audio, and video, into its AI models, enabling them to understand and generate content that spans multiple forms of media.

Reasoning and Common Sense: Meta is researching ways to enhance the reasoning and common sense capabilities of its AI models, enabling them to understand and respond to more complex and nuanced situations.

Personalized Language Models: Meta is exploring the development of personalized language models that adapt to individual users' communication styles and preferences, creating more natural and engaging interactions.

AI for the Metaverse

Meta's vision for the metaverse, a shared virtual world where people can interact and experience things together, relies heavily on AI. Meta is developing AI technologies to:

Create Realistic Avatars: AI can be used to create realistic and expressive avatars that accurately represent users in the metaverse.

Generate Immersive Environments: AI can generate realistic and dynamic virtual environments, from bustling cityscapes to serene natural landscapes.

Facilitate Social Interactions: AI can facilitate natural and engaging social interactions in the metaverse, enabling people to connect and communicate in new ways.

Power Virtual Assistants: AI can power intelligent virtual assistants that can guide users through the metaverse, provide information, and assist with tasks.

AI for Social Good

Meta is committed to using AI for social good, addressing global challenges and promoting positive social impact. This includes:

Accessibility: Meta is developing AI tools to improve accessibility for people with disabilities, such as real-time translation, image captioning, and text-to-speech conversion.

Misinformation and Hate Speech Detection: Meta is using AI to detect and remove harmful content, such as misinformation and hate speech, from its platforms.

Crisis Response: Meta is developing AI tools to assist in crisis response, such as identifying and filtering out misinformation during natural disasters or public health emergencies.

Environmental Sustainability: Meta is using AI to optimize energy consumption, reduce waste, and promote sustainable practices in its operations and across its platforms.

Ethical and Responsible AI Development

Meta is committed to developing AI responsibly and ethically, addressing concerns about bias, fairness, and privacy. This includes:

Investing in Responsible AI Research: Meta continues to invest in research to address key challenges in responsible AI, such as bias detection, fairness-aware algorithms, and explainable AI.

Promoting Transparency and Accountability: Meta is committed to transparency in its AI development and deployment, providing information about how its AI systems work and addressing concerns about potential harms.

Engaging with the Broader Community: Meta actively engages with the broader AI community, collaborating with researchers, policymakers, and civil society organizations to promote responsible AI practices and address ethical considerations.

The Future of Meta's AI

Meta's AI journey is an ongoing exploration of the frontiers of artificial intelligence. The company is committed to pushing the boundaries of AI research and development, creating AI that is innovative, responsible, and beneficial to humanity.

The future of Meta's AI involves:

Continuously Expanding Capabilities: Meta will continue to enhance the capabilities of its AI systems, improving language understanding, generating more realistic and creative content, and expanding into new domains like the metaverse.

Prioritizing Ethical Considerations: Meta will continue to prioritize ethical considerations in its AI development, addressing concerns about bias, fairness, and privacy, and ensuring that its AI systems are used responsibly.

Promoting Social Good: Meta will continue to explore ways to use AI for social good, addressing global challenges and promoting positive social impact.

By embracing innovation, responsibility, and a human-centered approach, Meta is shaping a future where AI empowers individuals, strengthens communities, and contributes to a better world for all.

9.2 Emerging Trends: The Evolution of Language Models

The field of large language models (LLMs) is a hotbed of innovation, with new architectures, training techniques, and applications emerging at a breakneck pace. This chapter explores the exciting trends shaping the evolution of language models, offering a glimpse into the future of this rapidly advancing field.

1. Beyond Scale: Efficiency and Optimization

While the trend of building ever-larger language models continues, there's a growing emphasis on efficiency and optimization. Researchers are exploring techniques to achieve comparable performance with smaller models that require less computational power and are more environmentally friendly. This includes:

Parameter-Efficient Fine-Tuning: Techniques like adapters and prompt tuning allow for adapting large language models to specific tasks with minimal changes to the model's parameters, reducing computational costs and improving efficiency.

Knowledge Distillation: This involves training smaller "student" models to mimic the behavior of larger "teacher" models, achieving comparable performance with reduced computational overhead.

Pruning and Quantization: These techniques involve removing unnecessary connections or reducing the precision of numerical representations within the model, leading to smaller and more efficient models.

2. Multimodality: Integrating Diverse Data

Language models are moving beyond text, embracing multimodal learning that incorporates diverse data types, such as images, audio, and video. This enables LLMs to:

Understand and Generate Richer Content: Multimodal LLMs can generate image captions, summarize video content, and even create new forms of media that combine text, images, and sound.

Ground Language in the Real World: By incorporating visual and auditory information, LLMs can better understand the context of language and generate more grounded and relevant responses.

Create More Interactive Experiences: Multimodal LLMs can power more interactive and immersive experiences, such as virtual assistants that can understand and respond to both spoken language and visual cues.

3. Enhanced Reasoning and Problem-Solving

Researchers are actively working on enhancing the reasoning and problem-solving abilities of LLMs. This involves developing new architectures and training techniques that enable LLMs to:

Perform Logical Deduction: LLMs are being trained to perform logical reasoning tasks, such as solving puzzles, answering questions that require inference, and even generating mathematical proofs.

Exhibit Common Sense: Infusing LLMs with common sense knowledge is a key challenge. Researchers are exploring ways to incorporate knowledge graphs, commonsense reasoning datasets, and even human feedback to improve LLMs' understanding of the world.

Solve Complex Problems: LLMs are being applied to complex problem-solving tasks, such as scientific discovery, drug development, and even code generation.

4. Personalization and Customization

LLMs are becoming increasingly personalized, adapting to individual users' needs and preferences. This trend is driven by:

Fine-tuning on User Data: LLMs can be fine-tuned on individual user data, such as their writing style, interests, and communication patterns, to create more personalized and engaging experiences.

Adaptive Learning: LLMs can adapt their responses and behavior based on user interactions, learning their preferences and providing more relevant and helpful information.

User-Generated Content: LLMs can be trained on user-generated content, such as social media posts and online reviews, to better understand and respond to individual users' needs.

5. Ethical and Responsible AI

As LLMs become more powerful and pervasive, ethical considerations are taking center stage. This includes:

Bias Mitigation: Researchers are developing techniques to identify and mitigate biases in LLMs, ensuring that they do not perpetuate harmful stereotypes or discriminate against certain groups.

Explainability and Interpretability: Making LLMs more explainable and interpretable is crucial for building trust and ensuring accountability. Researchers are developing techniques to understand how LLMs make decisions and provide insights into their reasoning processes.

Safety and Robustness: Ensuring the safety and robustness of LLMs is crucial for preventing unintended consequences and malicious use. Researchers are developing techniques to make LLMs more resilient to adversarial attacks and ensure that they behave as intended.

LLaMA's Place in the Evolving Landscape

LLaMA, with its open-source nature and focus on research, is well-positioned to contribute to these emerging trends. Its accessibility allows researchers to experiment with new architectures, training techniques, and applications, pushing the boundaries of LLM capabilities.

By fostering collaboration, transparency, and ethical considerations, LLaMA is helping to shape a future where LLMs are not only powerful but also responsible, beneficial, and accessible to all.

9.3 LLaMA and the Metaverse: Building Immersive Experiences

The metaverse, a persistent and shared virtual world where people can interact, create, and explore, is rapidly becoming a reality. And AI, particularly language models like LLaMA, is poised to play a pivotal role in shaping this immersive digital realm. This chapter explores the exciting intersection of LLaMA and the metaverse, examining how this powerful language model can contribute to building richer, more engaging, and personalized virtual experiences.

LLaMA: The Architect of Virtual Worlds

LLaMA's ability to understand and generate human language makes it a versatile tool for creating and interacting with the metaverse. Here are some key ways LLaMA can contribute:

World Building and Content Creation: LLaMA can generate descriptions of environments, objects, and characters, helping developers populate virtual worlds with rich and diverse content. Imagine describing a fantastical landscape to LLaMA and having it generate detailed descriptions of lush forests, towering mountains, and hidden caves, complete with unique flora and fauna.

Interactive Storytelling: LLaMA can power interactive narratives within the metaverse, generating dynamic storylines, personalized dialogues, and even branching paths based on user choices. This allows for immersive storytelling experiences where users actively participate in shaping the narrative.

Creating Non-Player Characters (NPCs): LLaMA can be used to create more realistic and engaging NPCs that can converse naturally with users, respond to questions, and even exhibit unique personalities and behaviors. This can make virtual worlds feel more alive and immersive.

Personalized Experiences: LLaMA can analyze user preferences and tailor metaverse experiences to individual tastes. This could involve generating personalized quests, recommending activities, or even creating custom virtual environments based on user interests.

Enhancing Social Interaction in the Metaverse

LLaMA can also enhance social interaction within the metaverse, facilitating communication and fostering a sense of community:

Real-time Translation: LLaMA's multilingual capabilities can translate languages in real-time, allowing users from different linguistic backgrounds to communicate seamlessly within the metaverse.

Accessibility: LLaMA can generate text-to-speech and speech-to-text conversions, making the metaverse more accessible for people with disabilities.

Moderating Conversations: LLaMA can be used to moderate conversations, identify and filter out toxic language, and promote positive interactions within the metaverse.

LLaMA and Virtual Assistants

LLaMA can power intelligent virtual assistants that can guide users through the metaverse, provide information, and assist with tasks. These assistants can:

Answer Questions: LLaMA can answer questions about the metaverse, its features, and its inhabitants, providing users with the information they need to navigate and explore this digital world.

Provide Recommendations: LLaMA can recommend activities, events, and places to visit based on user preferences and interests, enhancing their metaverse experience.

Assist with Tasks: LLaMA can assist with tasks such as creating avatars, customizing virtual environments, and even purchasing virtual goods and services.

Challenges and Opportunities

While LLaMA offers exciting possibilities for building immersive metaverse experiences, there are also challenges to address:

Computational Resources: Running LLaMA in real-time within the metaverse can require significant computational resources. Optimizing LLaMA for efficiency and leveraging cloud computing infrastructure will be crucial.

Ethical Considerations: As with any AI application, it's important to address ethical considerations, such as bias in language models, data privacy, and the potential for misuse.

User Experience: Designing user interfaces and interactions that seamlessly integrate LLaMA's capabilities into the metaverse experience will be crucial for user adoption and satisfaction.

The Future of LLaMA and the Metaverse

The future of LLaMA and the metaverse is filled with potential. As both technologies continue to evolve, we can expect even more immersive, engaging, and personalized virtual experiences.

Imagine a metaverse where you can converse naturally with AI-powered characters, explore dynamic and personalized worlds, and participate in interactive narratives that respond to your choices. This is the future that LLaMA is helping to build, a future where the boundaries between the physical and digital worlds blur, and where human creativity and AI intelligence converge to create truly immersive and transformative experiences.

Chapter 10

The Llama Effect: A Conclusion

10.1 The Transformative Power of AI: A Recap

As we conclude our exploration of LLaMA and its impact on the world, it's essential to take a step back and reflect on the broader transformative power of AI. Throughout this book, we've witnessed how AI is reshaping industries, accelerating scientific discovery, enhancing creativity, and redefining the very nature of human communication.

Let's recap the key takeaways and look towards a future shaped by this revolutionary technology.

AI is Democratizing Access to Powerful Tools

One of the most significant impacts of AI is its ability to democratize access to powerful tools and technologies. LLaMA, with its open-source nature, exemplifies this trend. By making advanced AI models accessible to researchers, developers, and even hobbyists, AI is empowering individuals and communities to innovate, create, and solve problems in ways never before imagined.

AI is Amplifying Human Capabilities

AI is not here to replace humans; it's here to augment our capabilities and help us achieve more. From automating mundane tasks to providing creative inspiration and accelerating scientific discovery, AI is freeing us from limitations and empowering us to reach new heights of productivity, creativity, and innovation.

AI is Reshaping Industries and the Future of Work

AI is transforming industries across the board, from healthcare and education to manufacturing and customer service. While this transformation brings challenges, such as the need for workforce adaptation and reskilling, it also creates new opportunities for collaboration, innovation, and the development of uniquely human skills.

AI is Fostering Connection and Understanding

AI is changing how we connect, communicate, and build relationships. From breaking down language barriers to combating social isolation, AI is fostering understanding and empathy, creating a more connected and inclusive world.

AI is Driving Scientific Discovery

AI is accelerating scientific discovery, helping researchers analyze vast amounts of data, generate hypotheses, and explore new frontiers of knowledge. From drug discovery and genomics to climate science and materials science, AI is driving progress and unlocking new possibilities for understanding the universe and improving human lives.

AI is Challenging Us to be More Ethical and Responsible

The rise of AI presents ethical challenges that require careful consideration and responsible action. From addressing bias and fairness to protecting privacy and ensuring accountability, we must navigate these challenges to ensure that AI is used for the benefit of humanity and the advancement of a just and equitable society.

The Future of AI: A Collaborative Journey

The future of AI is not solely in the hands of tech giants or research labs; it's a collaborative journey that involves all of us. By embracing open-source principles, fostering ethical AI development, and promoting inclusivity and accessibility, we can shape a future where AI empowers individuals, strengthens communities, and contributes to a better world for all.

Embracing the Transformative Power of AI

As we move forward into an increasingly AI-driven world, let us embrace the transformative power of this technology while remaining mindful of its challenges and responsibilities. By fostering collaboration, innovation, and ethical AI development, we can harness the full potential of AI to create a future that is more prosperous, equitable, and sustainable for all.

10.2 Challenges and Opportunities: Navigating the Future of LLaMA and AI

The journey through the world of LLaMA and AI has revealed a landscape brimming with both immense potential and complex challenges. As we stand at the cusp of a new era defined by intelligent machines, it's crucial to navigate the future with wisdom, foresight, and a commitment to responsible innovation. This chapter explores the key challenges and opportunities that lie ahead, offering a roadmap for harnessing the transformative power of AI while mitigating its potential risks.

Challenges: Navigating the Ethical Landscape

The rapid advancement of AI presents a host of ethical challenges that require careful consideration and proactive solutions:

Bias and Fairness: AI models, including LLaMA, can inherit and amplify biases present in the data they are trained on. Addressing this requires developing fairness-aware algorithms, ensuring diverse and representative datasets, and promoting transparency and accountability in AI development.

Privacy and Security: Protecting privacy in the age of AI is paramount. This involves implementing robust data security measures, anonymizing data whenever possible, and empowering users with control over their information.

Misinformation and Malicious Use: The ability of LLMs to generate highly realistic and convincing content raises concerns about the spread of misinformation and the potential for malicious use, such as creating deepfakes or generating harmful content. Addressing this requires developing safeguards, promoting responsible use, and fostering media literacy.

Job Displacement and Economic Inequality: The automation potential of AI raises concerns about job displacement and the widening of economic inequality. Navigating this challenge requires investing in education and reskilling programs, promoting human-AI collaboration, and ensuring equitable access to AI opportunities.

Existential Risks: While still largely theoretical, the potential for advanced AI to surpass human intelligence raises long-term existential risks that require careful consideration and proactive planning.

Opportunities: Shaping a Better Future

Despite the challenges, AI offers immense opportunities to improve our lives and create a better future:

Accelerating Scientific Discovery: AI can accelerate scientific breakthroughs in fields like medicine, materials science, and climate change, leading to new treatments, sustainable solutions, and a deeper understanding of the universe.

Enhancing Creativity and Innovation: AI can augment human creativity, inspiring new ideas, automating tedious tasks, and enabling the creation of new forms of art, music, and literature.

Improving Education and Accessibility: AI can personalize education, enhance accessibility for students with disabilities, and empower educators with data-driven insights.

Promoting Social Connection and Understanding: AI can break down language barriers, combat social isolation, and foster empathy and understanding across cultures.

Addressing Global Challenges: AI can be used to address pressing global challenges, such as poverty, hunger, disease, and climate change, by optimizing resource allocation, developing sustainable solutions, and providing personalized interventions.

Navigating the Future: A Roadmap

To navigate the future of AI successfully, we need a roadmap that prioritizes responsible innovation, ethical considerations, and human-centered design:

Invest in Research and Development: Continued investment in AI research and development is crucial for addressing challenges, unlocking new possibilities, and ensuring that AI benefits all of humanity.

Promote Ethical AI Development: Establish clear ethical guidelines, promote fairness and transparency, and ensure accountability in AI development and deployment.

Foster Collaboration and Inclusivity: Encourage collaboration between researchers, policymakers, industry leaders, and the public to ensure that AI development is inclusive and benefits everyone.

Educate and Empower: Provide education and training on AI concepts, ethical considerations, and digital literacy to empower individuals and communities to participate in the AI era.

Embrace a Human-Centered Approach: Design AI systems that complement and augment human capabilities, rather than replacing them, and prioritize human well-being and societal benefit.

The Path Forward

The future of AI is not predetermined; it's a path we forge together. By embracing responsible innovation, ethical considerations, and a human-centered approach, we can navigate the challenges and opportunities that lie ahead, creating a future where AI empowers individuals, strengthens communities, and contributes to a better world for all.

10.3 Embracing the Change: LLaMA's Role in Shaping Our World

The rise of artificial intelligence, exemplified by powerful language models like LLaMA, marks a profound shift in our technological landscape. This is not merely a technological evolution; it's a societal one, with the potential to reshape how we live, work, and interact with the world around us. This final chapter emphasizes the importance of embracing this change, acknowledging both the challenges and opportunities that AI presents, and highlighting LLaMA's unique role in shaping a future that benefits all of humanity.

LLaMA: A Catalyst for Change

LLaMA, with its open-source nature, impressive capabilities, and focus on research, is a catalyst for change in the AI landscape. By democratizing access to powerful AI tools, LLaMA empowers individuals, communities, and organizations to innovate, create, and solve problems in unprecedented ways.

Embracing the Positive Transformations

LLaMA and AI are already transforming our world in positive ways:

Accelerating Scientific Discovery: From drug discovery and genomics to climate modeling and materials science, AI is accelerating research and driving breakthroughs that can improve human lives and address global challenges.

Enhancing Creativity and Productivity: AI is augmenting human creativity, automating tedious tasks, and enabling the creation of new forms of art, music, and literature. It's also boosting productivity in various industries, freeing up human workers to focus on more strategic and fulfilling tasks.

Improving Communication and Accessibility: AI is breaking down language barriers, enhancing accessibility for people with disabilities, and fostering more inclusive and empathetic communication.

Personalized Learning and Education: AI is personalizing the learning experience, tailoring education to individual needs, and providing students with the support they need to succeed.

Building a More Connected World: AI is connecting people across geographical and cultural boundaries, fostering understanding, and combating social isolation.

Navigating the Challenges

While embracing the positive transformations of AI, it's crucial to acknowledge and address the challenges:

Ethical Considerations: Bias, fairness, privacy, and accountability are paramount concerns that require ongoing attention and responsible AI development.

Workforce Adaptation: The automation potential of AI necessitates workforce adaptation and reskilling to prepare for the changing nature of work.

Equitable Access: Ensuring equitable access to AI technologies and opportunities is crucial to prevent a widening digital divide and ensure that AI benefits all of humanity.

LLaMA's Role in Shaping the Future

LLaMA, with its open-source nature and focus on research, is uniquely positioned to contribute to a positive future for AI:

Democratizing AI: LLaMA's accessibility empowers a broader community to participate in AI development and innovation, fostering a more diverse and inclusive AI ecosystem.

Promoting Transparency and Collaboration: LLaMA's open-source nature promotes transparency and collaboration, enabling researchers to identify and address potential biases, ethical concerns, and safety issues.

Accelerating Research and Innovation: LLaMA's capabilities and accessibility are accelerating research and innovation in various fields, leading to new discoveries and solutions that can benefit society.

Embracing Change, Shaping the Future

The rise of AI is a transformative force that is reshaping our world in profound ways. By embracing this change, acknowledging both the challenges and opportunities, and actively participating in shaping the future of AI, we can ensure that this powerful technology is used for the benefit of humanity and the advancement of a more just, equitable, and sustainable world.

LLaMA, as a catalyst for innovation and a symbol of open and collaborative AI development, is playing a pivotal role in this journey. Let us embrace the change, harness the power of LLaMA and AI, and work together to create a future where technology empowers individuals, strengthens communities, and unlocks the full potential of human ingenuity.

www.ingramcontent.com/pod-product-compliance
Lightning Source LLC
LaVergne TN
LVHW051739050326
832903LV00023B/997